David Pryde

The Queer Folk of Fife

Tales from the Kingdom

David Pryde

The Queer Folk of Fife
Tales from the Kingdom

ISBN/EAN: 9783744768511

Printed in Europe, USA, Canada, Australia, Japan

Cover: Foto ©ninafisch / pixelio.de

More available books at **www.hansebooks.com**

The Queer Folk of Fife:

Tales from the Kingdom

BY

DAVID PRYDE, M.A., LL.D.

AUTHOR OF "PLEASANT MEMORIES OF A BUSY LIFE"
"THE HIGHWAYS OF LITERATURE"
"GREAT MEN IN EUROPEAN HISTORY," ETC.

GLASGOW
MORISON BROTHERS
52 RENFIELD STREET
1897

CONTENTS.

	PAGE
THE BREACH OF PROMISE,	9
HER DEAD SELF,	33
GOD'S OWN SCHOLAR,	52
THE GENTLEMAN TRAMP,	84
THE ONE FATAL MISTAKE,	123
A ROMANCE OF THE HARVEST FIELD,	167
THE BOY HERETIC,	198
HOW THE DEACON BECAME AN ABSTAINER,	240

INTRODUCTION.

FIFTY years ago, the little burgh-town of Sandyriggs was a sleepy place. The inhabitants led, what they themselves called, "an easy-osy life." So little stir was there in the life of the small shopkeeper or tradesman, that he might be said to "vegetate." He grew and flourished where he had been born, and among his own schoolmates and his parents' cronies, who still called him by the fond familiar name of his boyhood, "Johnny," or "Jamie," or "Robby," as the case might be. His place of business was part of his home; and during the day he oscillated comfortably between the front shop and the back parlour. There was little competition, and very little anxiety about his trade. His customers were his friends, and he could rely implicitly on their support. It happened, therefore, that even in what he called his busiest time, he had many intervals of leisure during which he was at a loss what to do.

Of a similar complexion was the life of the small farmers who abounded in the neighbourhood. The farmer, or "gudeman," as he was called, toiled, it is true, in the fields by the side of his own servants; but he had little of the endless anxiety of the husbandmen of the present time. In those halcyon days of Protection, he was the especial care of the Lords and Commons of Great Britain and Ireland. They were his guardian angels. What did it matter to him though the drought burned up his turnips, and the drenching rains blackened his barley? The prices rose at once to guard him against loss. Consequently, after his day's "darg," and when he had exchanged his muddy boots for slippers, and taken his "four hours" of tea and buttered scones, he could sit down, snuff-box in hand and free from care, and take his ease by the side of the blazing kitchen fire. Thus the peasantry, like the townsfolk, had their intervals of leisure, during which they were open for any entertainment that might come before them.

Now, the important question came to be, How were these intervals of leisure to be filled up? There were no daily papers, few magazines, and few books to satisfy their craving for knowledge. Their minds were, therefore, obliged to feed upon the gossip of the country side; and so it came about that the gift of story-telling was cultivated, and that there were men and women who were recognised as the chroniclers of the district. These were the public entertainers, and were constantly called upon to use their gifts, especially for the delight of the young.

Two of these chroniclers, a couple of the name of Steedman, I chanced to know. Better samples of "auld-farrant Scotch bodies" could not be imagined. In no other habitat than a quaint burgh like Sandyriggs could they have grown up. For many years they had "gathered gear" in a grocer's "shoppie," and had then retired on a competence. They now lived in a cottage, crooked, grey, and time-worn like themselves. A favourite niece waited upon them, for they preferred, after the patriarchal fashion, to be served by their own kith and kin, and not by the *frem'd*. Their religion, too, was of the olden type. They were Original Seceders, would not enter an Established Church, travelled miles to attend a Dissenting Chapel, believed every iota of the Bible and the Confession of Faith, kept the Sabbath strictly, abhorred novels as "parcels o' lees," and looked upon food that had not been consecrated by a long grace as absolute poison. Yet their religion, straight-laced though it might be called, did for them what more fashionable religions sometimes fail to do for their adherents. It made them far more cheerful, and far more appreciative of the blessings of life. The snow of winter was on their head, but the warmth of summer was in their heart. A brighter, *cantier*, and cosier pair could not be seen. They delighted in all their surroundings: their work, their religious exercises, their pipe of tobacco, and their nightly glass of toddy. They were particularly fond of recalling the scenes and incidents of the Past, and as I was an appreciative listener, I was always a welcome guest, and in fact was invited to drop in upon them as often as I could.

As I write, the old couple are before me, one on each side of the hearth—he, in a brown suit with a cloth cap covering his grey hair, and with a most intelligent countenance—she, a tidy little body, with clean-cut features and with coloured ribbons in her cap—he, recalling with unction some bygone event—she, interpolating occasionally to add some little detail to complete the narrative—and both radiant with pleasure, as if the light of other days were warming their hearts and brightening their faces.

"What a blessing," he would say, "is a good memory—one of the most precious gifts of God."

After the fashion of old people, they often repeated the stories which they had told me on former occasions; but I did not object, as I was thus enabled to realise them more thoroughly.

Some of the scenes and incidents which I acquired in this way, I now proceed to give as truthfully and clearly as I can.

THE BREACH OF PROMISE.

AFTER a long dearth of news, an event happened to revive the interest of the gossips of Sandyriggs. That snug, substantial villa, Townhead Lodge, which stood within a garden, large and sloping to the south, had got at last a tenant, a Mr Callendar, whose family consisted of a wife, a son, and two daughters. And what was most interesting, there was a mystery about them all! Where they had come from, what was the source of their income, and why they kept themselves apart, no one knew.

The father drove a gig of his own and was often from home. The mother was a recluse, and rarely ventured beyond her own walls. But the one who attracted the most notice was the elder daughter, who was frequently seen in the streets of the town attended by her brother. She was a mere girl of sixteen or seventeen, but she was exceedingly beautiful. Regarding

B

her special charms, I never could learn much, except that she had a straight and lissome figure, dark hair, clear blue eyes, and a modest and winning expression, and above all that she had a sort of glamour about her which bewitched everyone who looked at her. The family altogether seemed so distinguished, and at the same so mysterious, that the gossips of the town were all agog to know more about them. But how was this knowledge to be got? The newcomers were evidently bent on keeping themselves aloof, and having as little to do as possible with the natives. There was difficulty even in approaching them.

The one who overcame this difficulty was the late minister's sister, Miss MacGuffog, or, as she was familiarly called, "Miss Phemie." During the lifetime of her brother, who was a bachelor, she had taken a motherly interest in all the parishioners, and went out and in among them like a blood relation. After her brother's death, she kept up the practice. Uncharitable people sneered at her as a busybody; but they might have spared their sneers. They might have known that a busybody is not necessarily bad. It was not selfish curiosity, but kindly interest that was her motive. She was not a scandalmonger, but a sympathetic friend.

Having a high idea of everything connected with her brother's parish, she was prepared to find good everywhere, and generally found it. As a matter of course, it had been her custom to call upon strangers in order to give them a hearty welcome. In this way she came to know all that was to be known about the Callendars; and as she held it to be selfish and unneighbourly to keep anything to herself, she freely communicated her information to the town gossips who met over afternoon tea.

The information which she had gathered was as follows:—Mr Callendar was a partner in a firm of English merchants who did a large business all over the kingdom, and he had come to Scotland to establish a connection in Fife. Mrs Callendar was somewhat of an invalid, and passed the most of her time in reading. The elder daughter, Phoebe, was evidently the pride of her life. "Isn't she handsome and graceful," the mother had said as she fondly watched her going out of the room, "and would she not look at home in the highest mansion in the land?" It was evident that they expected her to make a great marriage.

Meanwhile Miss Callendar's transcendent loveliness was seriously affecting the male population of the village. What was afterwards called "the Callendar fever" broke out among the bachelors, both old and young. And during their fits of delirium they behaved most absurdly. One began laboriously to train a moustache; another shaved off his beard to show the fine lines of his face; another allowed his hair to grow till it fell in ringlets on his shoulders; while gouty Major Mustard (half-pay) dyed the tuft on his chin, and, looking into his mirror, said, "Begad! I don't think that she can refuse an officer of the British Army."

But the one who had the epidemic in the most aggravated form was Charles Raeburn, the town lawyer, and the laird of the small estate of Cowslip Brae. Charles was nothing if not poetical; and his ravings about Miss Callendar took the form of quotations from his favourite bards. He compared her to Spenser's Una, to Shakespeare's Portia drawing suitors from the four quarters of the world, to Virgil's Venus descending upon earth to fascinate mankind. One day (oh, ecstasy!) she came into his office to make some inquiries for the information of her father; but (oh, horror!) he lost his head, and gave the information in such an incoherent manner that she had some difficulty in understanding him. He wished to appear to her as a man of genius; but he had conducted himself like an idiot. All that he could do after this, was to wander round her house on moonlight nights, like a silly moth (as someone said) fluttering round a wax candle, or like a forlorn planet (as he himself said) circling round a central luminary. At length, his cousin, Dr Raeburn, thought to bring him to his senses by rating him soundly and telling him plainly that he was "carrying on like a lunatic." And, to the doctor's utter astonishment, Charles agreed with him.

"Yes," said the poor fool, "you are quite right. I *am* a lunatic — a monomaniac. I'm haunted by one idea, one image. It appears in my dreams. It fills my waking hours. Position, friends, relations, are dross compared with her. I would rather have her than the largest estate, than a whole county, than a continent, than a bright new planet all to myself."

But it was in the church on Sunday where the hopeless infatuation of the young men of the town was noticed. During the whole of the service, their eyes were fixed upon this young girl. Her pew was the pulpit, and she herself was both the preacher and the sermon. And one Sunday a strange phenomenon happened. The church, which was dingy and dark even at midsummer, appeared to be lighted up in some mysterious way. How came this to pass? On the previous Sunday, one of the many rivals, in order to attract the eyes of his goddess, had appeared in white waistcoat and white necktie; and all the others had lost no time in following suit.

How did Miss Callendar conduct herself under all this idolatry? Most modestly. When she appeared on the streets with her little brother by her side, she saluted everybody with a good-natured smile. She smiled on Major Mustard, and set his well-worn heart palpitating. She also smiled on Peter Samuel the mercer's apprentice, when coming into the shop unexpectedly she asked to see some gloves; and when Peter shook all over while he was showing her the gloves, and answered confusedly, she smiled still more sweetly.

" Bright as the sun her eyes all gazers strike,
And like the sun they shine on all alike."

One Sunday there appeared in the church a stranger, like a being from another sphere. That he was an aristocrat was evident. He had an elegant figure, clean-cut features, and easy manners; and, as Peter Samuel remarked, "was dressed up to the nines, and looked as if he had come out of a bandbox." In fact, he was a regular London-made exquisite, "a dandy," "a swell." Nor was there any mistake about the object of his visit. All during the service his eyes were fixed on Phoebe Callendar, the village beauty. That evening, too, in the Orchard Lane he was seen walking with her. Her little brother, indeed, was there. But the exquisite, with that ease which high society gives, and which local beaux can never acquire, was looking into her face and talking, while she blushed and held down her head. In a few days she disappeared. Had she eloped? Sandyriggs was in a ferment.

At last Miss Phemie MacGuffog solved the mystery. Miss Callendar's young lover was the heir to a dukedom. Her parents, alarmed at the intimacy, and thoroughly disapproving of it, had sent her to a boarding-school in England; and she was never seen again in Sandyriggs. In a few months the family gave up their house and departed southwards.

The one who was most affected by Miss Callendar's departure was Charles Raeburn. He grew melancholy, lost his appetite and his sleep, and wandered about like a ghost. He was like the traveller, when the moon, which has lightened and beautified his path over hill and dale, suddenly goes down and leaves him to stumble on in the dark. In a short time he vanished; and when months elapsed without bringing any intelligence regarding him, his neighbours gave him up for lost.

A few years passed, and the inhabitants had almost forgotten the Callendars, when they were startled by a short paragraph in the county newspaper, to the effect that Miss Phoebe Callendar was about to bring an action for breach of promise of marriage against the Duke of ——. Here was an interesting subject to talk about! A breach of promise against a duke by a former inhabitant of Sandyriggs, a girl whom they all knew! The whole district was in a flutter of excitement. When the trial came on in London, the editor of the *County Chronicle* employed a special correspondent to give a report of it; and when the newspaper containing the account of the trial arrived, it was devoured with breathless interest, and handed about from house to house.

After describing the appearance of the Court, and naming the famous barristers and attorneys employed on both sides, the reporter went on to say that the plaintiff, seated in a prominent place beside her legal advisers, was "the cynosure of every eye," and her exquisite beauty, and modest but melancholy expression, captivated at once not only the ordinary onlookers, but even the gentlemen of the jury themselves.

"The Attorney-General stated her case with all that romantic and touching eloquence for which he is famous. 'The plaintiff,' he said, 'was a young lady of the greatest personal attractions. When first she drew the attention of the defendant, she was living in retirement at the small town of Sandyriggs in Fife. She was a mere girl, attending to her lessons under the watchful care of her mother, and thinking of nothing but her daily duties and her innocent amusements. She was, indeed, the life of her parents' hearts, the idol of her young companions, and the delight and pride of the whole village.

But this golden age was not to last long; into this innocent paradise the serpent was soon to find his way. The defendant, then the Honourable Algernon Colenutt, an Oxford student, happened to be spending his vacation at a mansion in the neighbourhood. He heard of this charming young creature—this beauty of Sandyriggs, as she was called,—and he resolved to see her. It was no mere idle curiosity. He was one of those golden youths who think that everything is made for their amusement, that women especially are but toys that may be played with for a time, and then cast aside for ever.'

"'On a particular Sunday this gay Lothario attended the Sandyriggs church. His presence there was noticed by most of the congregation; and it was particularly remarked that his eyes were upon Miss Callendar during the whole service, and that, in fact, he was completely spellbound. Then in the evening he was seen talking to her in a lane near her own house. He had waylaid her, and it was then, it seems, that he gained her affections. By such a lover— young, handsome, aristocratic, elegant in dress and manners, polished in speech and adroit in flattery—was it surprising that the simple country maiden was won? Ere they parted she plighted her troth to him; and, proud of her conquest, the poor girl lost no time in making her mother her confidante.'

"'Now, Gentlemen of the Jury, you will very likely be told by my learned brother, the counsel for the defence, that Miss Callendar's parents were artful schemers, using every device to entrap an unwary nobleman. But what did they do as soon as they heard of this courtship? They immediately sent their daughter away to a boarding-school in England, and afterwards to France, to be out of the way of this aristocratic wooer. They were too sensible not to see that such a connection would be unequal, and likely to prove dangerous to the happiness of both parties. But their precautions were unavailing. The defendant was not to be denied. He contrived to find out where his beloved was, and to continue the correspondence; and after he had succeeded to the dukedom, and after the Callendars had settled down in England, at Woodhurst, about sixty miles from his ducal castle, his attentions became more assiduous. He visited her at her father's house, and sent many letters,—some of which I now produce,—

and all of which are full of the warmest protestations and the most endearing terms of affection. At length the wedding was fixed for July, and Miss Callendar and her mother set themselves to make all the necessary preparations. Up to this time, there had not been the slightest hitch, the slightest misunderstanding, and the happiness of the young couple seemed to be assured. But ere the appointed day arrived, what was the consternation of the Callendars to read in the newspaper the announcement that the Duke of —— had been married to Miss Fortescue Devlin. At first they could not believe the statement; but after inquiry they found that it was only too true. And, Gentlemen of the Jury, I can only leave you to imagine what a disastrous effect this sudden perfidy has had on my client. Her loving heart has been broken, and her fair young life has been for ever blighted.'

"'I believe that my learned brother is to take up the bold and desperate position that these facts are not true, and that the written correspondence is a forgery. What! a young, timid, and unsophisticated girl sitting down deliberately to forge, not one letter, but a whole bundle of letters, and doing it so accurately that she has deceived those who are best acquainted with the defendant's handwriting! Why, Gentlemen, the idea is preposterous, it is inconceivable, it is wholly and absolutely ridiculous!' (Derisive laughter, which was immediately suppressed.)

"The Attorney-General then proceeded to call witnesses in order to prove his statements. The sister of the plaintiff told that she had seen the defendant several times at her father's house, and in the company of her sister, and mentioned one occasion particularly, the 20th of May, which she had good cause to remember, because it was the fair day at the neighbouring village of Woodhurst, and the defendant presented her with a sovereign as a fairing. The mother gave evidence as to the receiving of the defendant's letters, and about her daughter's letters in reply being posted. An old clergyman, who had been the defendant's tutor, swore that the handwriting of the letters was that of his former pupil. These witnesses were severely cross-examined, but their evidence on the whole remained unshaken.

"Then Mr Ridley, the counsel for the Duke, arose. He was famous as a defender of abandoned criminals, and generally as a cunning handler of the most desperate cases. It was no uncommon thing for him to bully witnesses, and browbeat even the judge himself. Everybody, therefore, expected strong statements from him, but few were prepared for the merciless terms which he now used. Standing up, and looking round with a confident, triumphant air, he began his speech. 'The Attorney-General,' he said, 'in referring to the ground which was to be taken up for the defence, had scouted the idea of such a young and delicate creature perpetrating forgery. But my learned friend ought to know that in the history of crime there have been young girls as delicate and as refined as the plaintiff, who have been guilty of this heinous offence. I have only to refer to the cases of Elizabeth Canning and Mary Glen. In spite, therefore, of what the learned Attorney-General has said, I now assert, and am prepared to prove, that the plaintiff, guileless and modest as she looks, has perpetrated one of the most daring and elaborate forgeries in the whole of our criminal history.'

"At this assertion, uttered in a slow, distinct, and severe tone, Miss Callendar burst into tears, and was so completely overcome that she had to leave the Court. Cries of 'Shame, shame,' were hurled at the head of the counsel. But he, nothing abashed, looked round defiantly, and repeated the phrase with greater incisiveness; and went on in the same remorseless way to maintain that his client had scarcely ever seen Miss Callendar, had scarcely ever spoken to her, had scarcely ever written to her, and had certainly never made any promise of marriage. The audience glanced occasionally at the Attorney-General to see what effect this flat denial of all his assertions would have upon him; but he remained quite calm, just as if nothing unusual had been said.

"Mr Ridley then proceeded to examine his witnesses in the same peremptory style; and ever as he drew from them some important bit of evidence, he gave a triumphant look at the jury, as much as to say, 'What do you think of that? Wasn't what I told you true?' One was made to confess that the defendant had never seen Miss Callendar since his accession to the title; another, that the letters which had been read swarmed with ridiculous errors as to matter of fact; and another, that the handwriting was totally unlike that of the defendant. These witnesses were cross-examined, but took care not to contradict themselves. At all this, Miss Callendar's partisans, of whom there were many amongst the audience, were puzzled and even confounded; but an audible whisper, 'they are all relatives, and have got up the story,' restored their confidence. It was evident, too, that the Attorney-General felt that something was wrong; because he turned round to talk with the agent. But the audience was again perplexed by what followed.

"An innkeeper from Welldon, fifty miles from Woodhurst, was put into the box. In answer to examination, he said, 'that he knew the Duke of ——; that on the 20th of May, the day of Woodhurst Fair, and the day when he was said to have been at the house of the plaintiff, the Duke arrived in a post-chaise on his way to Market Bruton; that there could be no mistake about this, for here were the receipts for the post horses.' And these receipts were handed to the jury to examine.

"But the most startling bit of evidence was yet to come. A young lady entered the witness-box, kissed the Book, and was subjected to the following questioning:—(*Q*.) You are Miss Ironside? (*A.*) Yes. (*Q.*) You live at Woodhurst? (*A.*) I do. (*Q.*) You know the plaintiff? (*A.*) I do. (*Q.*) You remember a ball taking place at Lyndcaster? (*A.*) I do. (*Q.*) What was the date? (*A.*) Last year, in the month of April. (*Q.*) Who went with you to the ball? (*A.*) Miss Phoebe Callendar. (*Q.*) How was she dressed? (*A.*) In white, with one red rose in her hair. (*Q.*) Was there any person that she wished particularly to see at the ball? (*A.*) The Duke of ——. (*Q.*) How did you know that? (*A.*) She told me. (*Q.*) Look at that letter. Do you know the handwriting? (*A.*) Yes. (*Q.*) Whose is it? (*A.*) Miss Callendar's. (*Q.*) You are sure? (*A.*) Quite sure. Then Mr Ridley, turning to the jury, said he would read the letter, which was as follows:—

"'*April* 18.

"' MY DEAR LORD DUKE,—I hope that you will excuse a stranger giving you a bit of information which may be for your advantage. You are, I understand, going to the public ball at Lyndcaster. Well, you will see there a young lady to whom you lost your heart some years ago, and who has remained constant to you ever since. She is more graceful and beautiful than ever, and fit to be the bride of a prince. You will recognise her at once, for she will be dressed in white, with a red rose stuck in her raven hair.—I am, my dear Lord Duke, your sincere well-wisher.

"This letter fell upon the audience like a bombshell, and created the greatest excitement and consternation. But it was evident from the whispers of 'got up,' and 'bribed by the relations,' that the audience had not even yet given up Miss Callendar. And they were very much relieved when they saw the Attorney-General rise. He was evidently going to put a stop to this wholesale slander and forgery. Alas, however, for their hopes! Instead of hearing him expose the evidence that was being given, they heard him make an admission that has very seldom been made in a court of law. In a perfectly calm voice and manner he said that this letter had come upon them as a surprise, that they had neither the time nor the means of throwing any light upon it, and that, therefore, with the concurrence of his learned friends, the attorneys for the plaintiff, he now begged leave to withdraw from the contest. Under these circumstances the plaintiff would be non-suited. Accordingly the case was dismissed; the letter was impounded in order that Miss Callendar might be indicted for conspiracy; and the audience dispersed amid murmurs of astonishment. But it was noted that while the elder members of the crowd muttered their detestation of Miss Callendar's shameless forgery, the young men were louder than ever in their admiration."

"What a fascinating girl she must be," said one, "to be able to take in the sharpest attorneys and the most learned counsel at the bar! what a clever little witch!"

"By Jove," cried another, in a strong Irish accent, "she's too good for a duke's wife. She ought to be a queen. She *is* a queen, the queen of love and beauty, and should be classed with Helen of Troy, Cleopatra, and Mary Queen of Scots; and, bedad, it's meself that should loike to be Paris or Antony or Bothwell."

Next morning a note appeared in one of the London newspapers stating that Miss Callendar had been apprehended on a charge of forgery; but it was not true. She had vanished, and no one knew where she was.

Imagine the excitement now in Sandyriggs after this report had been read! The town became a fermenting vat of scandal. Whispers swarmed as fast as gnats in August, and, like gnats, they flew abroad and buzzed in the ears of the public. The case was discussed at every shop-counter, at every tea-table, at every street corner, in every public-house, on every turnip field. People who had never spoken to each other before, exclaimed as they passed each other, "Isn't this a dreadful affair?" And it was astonishing to find that everyone had foreseen, nay, had hinted such a catastrophe. So many people pose as true prophets after the fact!

Even Miss Phemie MacGuffog was forced to forego her usual charitable views, and to confess that the poor unfortunate girl had been ruined by her training. Every circumstance, she said, was against her. Her father was a worldly man, engrossed with money-making, and seldom at home. Her mother, a silly woman, was abandoned to romance reading, and neglected her everyday duties, and lived in a world of unreality. The poor girl herself got no solid education. She had no need, her mother told her, to be clever or accomplished. She was lovely, which was far better, and would undoubtedly make a grand match and be a titled lady. To look handsome, and graceful, and fascinating, therefore, was all that she required to do. And the despatching of her to a boarding-school, and then to the Continent, in order to escape her aristocratic admirer, was a mere device. She was sent to a boarding establishment near Oxford because *he* was a student there, and she afterwards went to France to continue her education because *he* had gone there. And Miss Phemie was told that the education which she received at both these places was of the flimsiest kind, being limited to the singing of one or two songs, the hammering out on the piano of one or two classical pieces, and the copying of one or two drawings. The most of the pupils' time and attention was devoted to talking about fine dresses, equipages, balls, and aristocratic admirers. "In fact," concluded Miss Phemie, "they were evidently taught to look upon the world, not as a sphere of duty and labour, but as a big *cookie shine.*"

The worthy people of Sandyriggs were still discussing this strange catastrophe, when a new surprise claimed their notice. Intelligence came regarding the long-lost Charles Raeburn. His cousin, the doctor, received a letter from him, bearing the postmark of a town in Spain, and empowering him to sell Cowslip Brae and transmit the price. Before the gossips had ceased to puzzle their brains over this extraordinary sacrifice, another letter arrived and explained the whole mystery. In the frankest and most straightforward language, Charles Raeburn told his cousin the following romantic tale:—

"I felt that I could not remain in Sandyriggs after the object of my adoration had gone. So I followed her to Oxford and to France, and back again to England, and was present at the trial. From my professional experience I very soon saw how judgment was likely to go, and what a terrible fate was hanging over the head of the unfortunate girl. So, when stung by Ridley's merciless language, she left the Court abruptly, I followed her, and in presence of her mother told her that the verdict was almost certain to be against her, and that, if it were so, she would be apprehended for forgery. While she stood aghast and dumb at this intelligence, I offered my assistance, and they accepted it. I went with them at once to their hotel, paid their bill, packed their luggage, and had everything ready for flight. As soon as the result which I had anticipated was announced, we were off, and by next morning were on the Continent. I took rooms for them in this town, and a lodging for myself not far off, and here we remained till we could see what ought to be done.

"One morning, Miss Callendar sent to say that she wanted to see me. When I went to her, she told me with tears in her lovely eyes that her mother must go back to her husband in England, but that she herself must remain abroad; and what could she do to earn her bread? Would I, the only friend she now had, advise her? What could I do but offer, as her husband, to protect and cherish her for the rest of her life. She started back in horror, declared that she was a criminal, a felon, a forger who ought to be in prison, and utterly unworthy to be the wife of an honest man, and that she would not bring disgrace on one whom she esteemed so much, whom—and here she gave way and cried most bitterly. Then there flashed through my brain and heart Spenser's exquisite lines:—

> "'Nought is there under heav'n's wide hollownesse
> That moves more deare compassion of mind
> Than beautie brought t' unworthy wretchednesse
> Through envy's snares, or fortune's freaks unkind.
> I, whether lately through her brightnesse blind,
> Or through alleageance and fast fealtie,
> Which I do owe unto all womankind,
> Feele my hart perst with so great agony,
> When such I see, that all for pity I could die.

"These were the very feelings that were thrilling through me. I lost control of myself. Dropping down on my knees and seizing her hand, I poured out my whole soul. What I said I cannot recall; but at last she reluctantly consented to marry me, on condition that I would do my very best to teach her to be a good woman and a dutiful wife. Poor brokenhearted darling, she was more sinned against than sinning. The persons really to blame were her mercenary father and her novel-reading mother, who neglected her education, and that hollow-hearted aristocrat who trifled with her innocence. And most touching it is to see how humble and yet how loving she is, and how her face is still 'combating with tears and smiles.' If she is not to be forgiven, there can be no such thing as forgiveness on earth. I am sure that I have done what is right. Away from her, I would have been in outer darkness. Beside her, I am in Paradise."

HER DEAD SELF.

THE narrative which I am about to give was a prime favourite at the winter firesides of the parish. Its chief incident is so extraordinary, that it has often been scouted as an improbability. But it is literally true, as may be ascertained by those who will take the trouble to investigate the chronicles of the period.

In the early years of the present century, the principal baker in Sandyriggs was Alister Gow. He had one son, Donald, and five daughters. The four elder girls, Flora, Ellen, Marjory, and Nora, were good-looking, with bright complexions and red cheeks; the youngest, Mysie, was plain, with irregular features and dingy colour. The four soon found husbands, thriving tradesmen in the place, who gave them what was called "a good setting down"; but no one came to court Mysie, and she remained at home to attend to the comfort of her parents, and specially to take charge of the shop.

"And when are you gaun aff, Mysie," said old Wull Spears, the most impudent man in the parish, "when are you gaun to be knocked doon to the highest bidder?"

"Oh!" said Mysie, in the bright manner peculiar to her, "I'm no in the market; there's nae demand for gudes like me."

"I wadna wonder," continued Wull, "that ye're gaun to be an auld maid."

"And what for no?" replied Mysie. "Maids, like Scotch whisky, improve by growin' auld."

The years rolled by and brought changes. While Mysie's married sisters, harassed by the ceaseless worries of housekeeping and child-rearing, became more and more careworn, Mysie herself, able and willing for all her duties, grew cantier and cantier every day. While they began to lose their good looks, she began to lose her plainness. The truth is, that she was, though probably she did not know it, a practical philosopher; and in a business-like manner she weighed the advantages and disadvantages of her lot.

"What have I kept," she said to herself, "by

remaining single? Good health, good spirits, home comforts, congenial employment, pleasant friends and neighbours. And what have I lost? A husband! And what is a husband? A pig in a poke, a lottery ticket that may take a prize but is far more likely to get a blank. If I'm not happy now, I never deserve to be."

So she resolved to keep a contented mind, to dwell on the blessings she had, and not on those which she had not, to make the most of her life, and to find something good in everything. She was cheerful under all circumstances, and had a smile and a kind word for all her fellow-creatures. As the old people expressed it, "she was everybody's body." However dull and cheerless the weather might be in the streets of the town, there was always sunshine in the baker's shop at the corner of Water Lane. And this genial, kindly disposition soon began to tell upon her own appearance. It actually cleared her complexion, brightened her eyes, and made her look (as an old woman remarked) "halesome, wicelike, and bonny." She became a walking proof of the truth of the proverb that "a kindly disposition is the best cosmetic." And thus it happened, that not only old people and children were attracted by her, but even wooers; and among them came (wonderful to relate) the dandy draper, the woman-killer, the gay Lothario of the town.

This was Bob Dallas. The worship of his mother and sisters had convinced him that he was an Adonis; and the bright smiles of the village maidens had confirmed this belief. "A' the lasses," his sisters would remark to a friend, "are in love wi' oor Bob;" and his mother, in her strong idiomatic Scotch, would add—"Toots, ye ken, they'll no lie aff 'im." Accordingly, he wore on his countenance a constant smirk of satisfaction, and he entered a company as if to the tune, "See the Conquering Hero comes." He sought female society to captivate, not to sue, to receive admiration, not to give it. A pretty girl was a plaything to be taken up for a short time, and then changed for something else. Some people called this conduct cruelty; but he thought it kindness. A smile from him, he believed, was a favour which every woman would prize.

It was this notorious flirt that now fixed his eye upon Mysie. She was different from the pink-and-white damsels with whom he had been accustomed to trifle; but it was this very difference that fascinated him. He began to "show her attention" at every opportunity, to walk home with her from church, and to go frequently to her shop in the evening. At first, Mysie was surprised and not a little amused. She joked with him, telling him that if he was often seen with her his many admirers would hate her, and, what would be more dreadful, his reputation as a judge of female beauty would be gone. And when, one evening after the shop was closed, he actually went the length of asking her to be his wife, she laughed outright in his face, and told him that he didn't know his own mind, that he would tire of her plain features in a fortnight, and that she could never be any more to him than a sincere well-wisher.

But when, like a spoilt child unaccustomed to be balked, he sulked and mooned about the streets with a pale and miserable face, and at the end of a few weeks sent her a frenzied letter, vowing that if he could not win her he would drown himself in the loch, she relented. She was too charitable to believe that he was not in dead earnest, and what could she do but ask him to call upon her? And when, dropping on his knees, he shed tears and vowed that she was the only one he had ever loved, the only one he would ever love, she yielded and promised to be his wife.

Mysie was now happier than ever. Though she had been quite content to remain single, she was delighted to have gained the exclusive devotion of a man. Though well able by herself to fight the battle of life, she felt that her happiness would be made more sure by having constantly by her side one whom she could call her own, her other self. There was also a special *éclat* in having won the prize which so many had in vain competed for.

"My certie," said Mrs Patullo, the minister's wife, when she looked in at the shop, along with her husband and her son Tom, to congratulate her, "my certie! it's something to have killed the Lady-killer."

"Yes! Mysie," said the minister, "you have caught and tamed the roving zebra of the desert, who has hitherto been thought untamable."

"Ay," added Master Tom, who had contracted the abominable habit of punning, "and you are now going to lead him to the *halter*."

Mysie set about preparing for her marriage in a business-like way. Very little time was spent in billing and cooing. An early day was fixed for the ceremony. A small house was taken, and suitable furniture ordered. And that she might have her trousseau ready in time, she called in her cousin, Bessie Gayley, to assist her. Bessie was a good-looking, bright damsel, ready with her tongue, with her wits, and with her hands,—up to anything, equal to any emergency. She made herself generally useful and agreeable, helped in the house and in the shop, and when Mysie was specially occupied of an evening, entertained Bob with her chit-chat.

It was just two days before the date fixed for the wedding. Mysie had closed the shop, and was sitting in the back parlour. She was alone, for her father and mother were in the kitchen, and Bessie and Bob had gone out on some errand of their own. She felt rather depressed,—a state which was very unusual with her, and which she could not account for. In a short time she heard Bob and Bessie come in. Then there occurred a few awful moments which she never forgot for the rest of her life, and which made her heart throb. First, there was an earnest whispering in the passage, then a strange silence, and at last the door opened. She rose instinctively to her feet, for she saw by their faces that some calamity had happened.

"What is it?" she exclaimed. "Why don't you tell me?"

Bessie looked at Bob as if urging him to speak, and Bob, blushing and stammering, said, "I'm very sorry, Mysie; but I can't help it. I like you very much, but I don't feel towards you as a husband should do. The fact is that Bessie and I have discovered that we were made for each other."

Mysie stared at them for a moment, thinking that it might possibly be a joke; but their guilty looks showed that it was a stern reality. Clutching the back of her chair, and mustering all her natural strength of character, she said, in a voice preternaturally calm:

"So, Mr Dallas, you have found out that you can't give me the affection of a husband! Well, I'll manage to do without it; and at any rate I'm glad that you have told me in time. As for you, you serpent in the form of a woman, I'll leave you to the punishment of your own conscience. And if you have not got such an article, as seems very likely, it will be punishment enough to be tethered for life to that fickle fool that stands beside you." So saying, she passed out of the room, leaving the pair standing with guilt-stricken countenances.

It is well known that the lower animals often attack and even torment one of their own kind when he is sick or wounded. A good deal of this bestial habit still lingers among men. When distress falls upon us, our friends often aggravate that distress. They do not know, perhaps, that they are doing it, but still they do it. Had Mysie been left to herself, her own good sense and courage would have buoyed her up, and enabled her to trample her sorrow under foot. But when she went abroad, people would not allow her to forget that sorrow. Those who were her friends condoled with her. Those who were not her friends stared at her. She felt that the town was in a buzz about her affairs. And at home the tormenting process was even worse. Her mother bemoaned the slight that had fallen on the family. Her brother breathed forth threatenings against the features and limbs of the culprit. Her father talked incessantly about raising an action for breach of promise. In vain she told her mother and brother that they would best keep up the family honour, not by bewailings and threatenings, but by looking as if they thought the rupture of the engagement a blessed release. In vain she told her father that legal proceedings were not to be thought of, and that while they might be a punishment to Dallas, they would be a far greater punishment to herself. Morning, noon, and night, the worrying went on.

At length her highly-strung nervous system, which had buoyed her up above all her other troubles, fairly broke down. She lost the power of sleeping. She lost her appetite. A strange nausea took possession of her, and everything grew distasteful, and life itself became an intolerable burden. From having been the embodiment of happy good-nature, she changed into a woe-begone hypochondriac. And people unknowingly aggravated her disease by expressing astonishment at her altered appearance, by telling her that she looked very ill, and by bursting forth afresh into recriminations against the man that had jilted her. Then there came a morning when her room was found empty, and a note upon the dressing-table told her parents that she could bear the atmosphere of Sandyriggs no longer, and that she was off to a place where no one knew her, and where she would have perfect peace.

Blank consternation fell upon the family. When they recovered a little, the brother swore that he would go and smash Dallas, the author of all their woe; and the mother's impulse was to run abroad and get sympathy and advice from her neighbours. But the father, with far more tact and knowledge of the world, insisted that the first thing to be done at all hazards, was to prevent any scandal. They must not of their own accord say anything about the matter, and if any question should be asked, they must answer that she had gone to a friend's for a complete rest. Meanwhile they must try to find her.

This was no easy task. The very fact that they could not talk about it prevented them from getting any assistance from the outside world. For two or three days the brother, Donald, under pretence of paying ceremonious calls, made the round of all their intimate friends and relatives in the neighbouring farm towns and villages; but every night he returned worn-out, and with a despairing shake of the head intimated that he had got no trace of the lost one.

Then there flashed into the father's mind the

thought that she would likely be in Edinburgh; and he wondered that it had never occurred to him before. Why, a large town was the very place where a person, sick of being stared at and worried by inquisitive neighbours, would find rest; and they had a cousin there in whose house she would very likely get a lodging. Accordingly, the father and son set out at once, crossed the Firth in the ferry-boat from Pettycur to Leith, and then walked up Leith Walk to Edinburgh. They went to the cousin's address in Broughton Street, but found that she had moved at the last term, and none of the neighbours could tell where she had gone. Wearied out and disheartened, they put up at a hotel at Greenside, where they both passed an anxious and a restless night.

Next morning, for want of a better plan, they resolved to look for Mysie in the thoroughfares, the father taking the New Town and the brother taking the Old Town. The unhappy old man spent most of the day in wandering up and down the streets, looking in vain amid the throng of strange and unsympathetic faces for those familiar kindly eyes that had been the light of his home. Jaded and perplexed, he had returned to his hotel in the early afternoon, when the landlord, whom he had taken into his confidence the night before, laid the advertisement sheet of a newspaper before him, and pointed to a paragraph headed "Found Drowned." He glanced rapidly over it, and to his horror saw that it was a description of his lost daughter. There could be no mistake. The age, the complexion, the features, the hair, all corresponded.

Like one stunned by a heavy blow on the head, the old man sat still for a moment. Then, driven by a feeling made up of hope and fear, he hurried to the police office in the High Street, all unconscious of the traffic that rumbled and buzzed around him. In a short time he found himself in the death-chamber, in presence of a prostrate and shrouded form, lying so terribly still and quiet; and in another second the face-cloth was removed, and his worst fears were realised. Yes! in the stiff waxen mask he recognised that countenance which had so lately been the joy of everyone who looked upon it. He stood gazing at it like a man in a trance, till his pent-up feelings found vent in tears. Then it was that there occurred a most extraordinary circumstance — what would be deemed incredible, were it not vouched for by the chroniclers of the time. The door opened, and, in company with his son, there appeared the very woman whose fate he was bewailing and whose dead form he was gazing upon. She came forward, and her face took on a look of intense surprise at what she saw.

"Father!" she exclaimed, "what's wrang wi' ye? And what's this? mercy! what's this? can it be me? No! and yet it's awfu' like, but, no! no! Father, that's no' me! this is me." And she took both his hands and kissed him, and in this way convinced him that she was his own daughter.

And who was this dead woman that was Mysie's double? The question was never answered. She went to a pauper's grave unclaimed by anyone.

And how had Mysie chanced to arrive just at the critical moment? This was explained by the brother. On returning to the hotel, Donald had seen the advertisement, and had surmised where his father had gone. Hurrying up the North Bridge, he saw his sister, whom he had been picturing as a corpse lying at the police office, coming to meet him in her usual dress and manner. For an instant he felt like one in a dream. Could it really be she? His next thought was that she had been in some way brought back to life, and was hurrying down to relieve their fears; and when he heard that she had never been in the police office, he told her about the advertisement, and the two together made all haste to see their father.

Mysie stood for some time gazing at the dead face, and feeling for that poor young creature, who was so like her, a sort of kinship. And as she gazed, she read herself a severe lesson. What was her own trouble, she thought, contrasted with the terrible fate that had befallen this unknown one? A small trouble indeed! To be cast off by a man who had proved himself unworthy of her! Not a trouble at all, but a blessed relief! And as these thoughts passed through her mind, her spirit rose with a sudden impulse and threw off the incubus of melancholy that had so long weighed it down; and she came away, leaving, as it were, her dead self behind her. And when, after staying for a month with her cousin, till the sensation caused by "the wonderful case of mistaken identity" subsided, she returned home and resumed her duties, she had recovered her health and good spirits.

Taking her place in the shop, she devoted herself to the helping of her parents and the serving of their customers. And when any of the more inveterate gossips referred to her late painful experiences, she would stop them short with a good-natured smile, and the remark—" that's an auld sang noo, and it's no' worth the mindin'." Everybody was delighted to see that she was her old self again.

"Why," said old Mrs Raeburn, the doctor's mother, "the toon wasna like itsel withoot ye."

One day the Rev. Mr Patullo, with his wife and son, called in, to welcome her on her return. "You see," said the minister, "I could not want you, Mysie. You are my best specimen of a cheerful practical Christian. You are as good as a sermon."

"My certie," said Mrs Patullo, "far more interesting than the most of sermons."

"Though rather *floury*," added Tom, pointing to her hands.

But the best proof that Mysie's good-natured equanimity was restored, was her treatment of her faithless lover, Bob Dallas. His scandalous treatment of her had brought him into disgrace. Many of his friends had cut his acquaintance.

Even his betrothed, Bessie Gayley, ashamed of herself and ashamed of him, had refused in the end to marry him. He was now completely humiliated, and when he met Mysie in the street soon after her return, he could not look her in the face. But Mysie was too good-natured and sensible to keep up any ill-feeling towards this weak creature. So, the next time that she saw him she said, "Good morning"; and by and by she got into the habit of stopping to have a chat with him. At the same time, she took care to keep his familiarity within proper bounds. When, encouraged by her frankness and deluded by his own conceit, he imagined that she was still in love with him, and actually had the infatuation to refer to past times, she caught him up at once.

"Mr Dallas! remember we are friends, nothing more. And as a friend let me give you this advice: Don't think of marrying in this country. One wife would not be enough for you. Go out to the Salt Lake City, and there, as soon as you are tired of one spouse, you will be able to take another. Or perhaps, you as well as myself are doomed to remain single. I am too ugly to be married; you are too good-looking. It would be selfish in anyone to monopolise a man who gives so much pleasure to all the girls in the place."

At the end of many years, Bob Dallas and Mysie Gow were respectively an old bachelor and an old maid.

Bob winced keenly under the marring finger of Time, and, by means of wig, paint, powder, and a jaunty manner, tried to hide its ravages and to make the people believe that he was still young. He did not convince the people; but it is said that, sometimes at least, he managed to convince himself. On one occasion, while talking about his infant nephew, he said, "he's a fine little fellow," and running his fingers through his luxuriant artificial locks, he added, "with a head of hair as thick and as black as my own." Consequently he was seen at every gay gathering, bearing himself like an Adonis, and paying assiduous attention to the young ladies; and when they, fooling him to the top of his bent, gathered round him and bandied compliments with him, he put on a youthful air and silently congratulated himself that he was still "Bob Dallas, the Invincible."

"An auld donnert eediot," said the indignant

Mrs Chatteris, the town-clerk's widow, "deckin' himsel up like an antic for the lasses to giggle at."

"You're too hard upon him," said her son Joe. "He's more useful than that. He's an old battered figurehead, used by the girls as a butt for practising their arrows on."

Mysie, on the other hand, received the first touches of age in the most cheerful spirit, and wore her grey hair like a becoming ornament, and made her wrinkles shine with good humour; and, as her years grew fewer, she tried more and more to fill them, with grateful feelings towards her Maker and kind words and deeds towards her fellow-creatures.

GOD'S OWN SCHOLAR.

MANY years ago a new class of preachers started suddenly up in the country. They were called the sensational school, and were not unlike a certain section of the clergy in the present day. Their motto seemed to be: "Catch the public, by dignified means if you can, but by all means catch the public." Their rules for doing this were these: "Choose as the subject of your sermon some prevalent vice; denounce it in the plainest and strongest language; threaten those who practise it, or even encourage it, with all the misery of this world and all the eternal woes of the next; draw your illustrations hot from ordinary life; if they are vulgar or grotesque, and excite a titter, never mind; one great end is gained if by any means they arouse the interest of the audience."

The most promising member of this school was the Rev. Jeremiah MacGuffog, the new parish minister at Sandyriggs. He took the most solemn view of his office. He was placed there, he felt, as an ambassador of the Most High to denounce the iniquities that were lifting their heads on every side. It was no time for smooth words. Like the martyred prophets and reformers of old, he must boldly face the transgressors, tell them of their sins in the most direct language, and warn them of the terrible doom that awaits them.

While he was a student in Glasgow, he had often heard that the most productive root of immorality in the rural districts was the Bothy System. Everyone seemed to condemn it, and not one word had been said in its defence. It was clearly his duty, therefore, to strike it down without delay. Accordingly, one Sunday not long after his settlement, he wound up his afternoon sermon with a most merciless attack upon the farmers.

"The farmers," he said, "are a most respectable class of men, and I am deeply grieved to be compelled to say anything to wound their feelings; but I am here to tell them that they are responsible for what I call *the running sore*, which is draining the life-blood of morality and religion in the rural districts. I refer to the Bothy System. You, my brethren, are really treating your fellow-men like your cattle. You lodge them in a dirty and uncomfortable outhouse, and leave them there to corrupt each other. Did I say that you treated them *like* your cattle? I should have said *worse* than your cattle. For you do not prepare food for them, you do not tie them up, you do not lock them in and prevent them from roaming abroad at night and falling into mischief. I am sorry that I am obliged to use strong language, but in the faithful discharge of my duty I am called upon to say that these bothies are nurseries of the infernal pit, and that you who keep them up are, though you may not know it, really serving the devil."

It would be impossible to describe the volcano of feeling which this onslaught roused within the souls of the farming population. They could scarcely keep their seats till the service was over; then, when they went out of church and took their way homewards in the grey winter dusk, the turmoil within them was almost too strong for expression; and for a time they could only vent it in such explosive epithets, as "nurseries o' the infernal pit!" "servants o' the deevil!"

"ill-tongued cratur!" "empty-headed puppy!" "set him up!" "my certie!" But by the time they reached the foot of the Long Dykes, where the road divided into three, a group of them, both men and women, stood still to compare notes.

"Sic a desecration o' the poopit!" said Mrs Dowie of Seggie Den; "instead o' preachin' the gospel, misca'in honest folk."

"Eh, woman!" exclaimed Mrs Caw of Blawearie, "ye may say that. Him to turn up his nose at bothies, that was brocht up, they tell me, in a one-roomed hoose in the wynds o' Glesky. My word, it doesna set a soo to wear a saddle."

"Low-born smaik," said Mrs Proud of the Hill, "to scandaleese his betters!"

"I dinna ken," said Tam Bluff of Cuddiesknowes, "what they teach them at college, but it's evidently no' mainners."

"Settin' servants against their maisters," said Stables, the horse doctor, a Tory of the old school.

"What could ye expect," asked Ure, the innkeeper at Blawearie Yetts, "from a teetotaller? Did ye hear hoo he blackguarded onybody that had onything to dae wi' makin' or sellin' an honest drap o' drink. Haith! it's my opinion that when the Maister comes to the warld a second time, they'll steek in His face the door o' His ain kirk, because He ance turned water into wine."

Then Manson of the Hole, who had been standing by, red with rage, now began to splutter forth his resentment. He was a cantankerous old bachelor, greedy, miserly, and wealthy. If any bothy in the neighbourhood deserved to be tabooed, it was his. That was the reason for his feeling the most aggrieved. "By the Lord Hairy," he said, "I'll astonish the dirty cratur. I'll hae a ring in his nose before he's a week aulder. I'll ceet him before the Presbytery, and if that wunna dae, before the Synod and the General Assembly; and if I canna get justice there, I'll gang to the Law. Don't ye think I'm richt, Gilbert Strang?"

The man who was thus addressed, and who now came up, was evidently somewhat inferior in station to the rest of the group. In fact, at first sight he looked shabby. His hat was weather-stained, his clothes were threadbare and even darned in some places, and his boots were rough and clumsy. But his well-developed figure, his clean-cut and healthy features, and his big blue eyes, gave him, in spite of his mean apparel, a look of superiority. Nay, the neat patches on his coat seemed, in some odd way, to be badges of respectability. He was the son of a small laird; but his father had recently died, a heartbroken bankrupt; the property had been sold; he had been left the sole support of his widowed mother, and had been obliged to hire himself out as an ordinary ploughman; and it was understood that he was now pinching himself to save money, in order, if possible, to redeem the little family inheritance.

Gilbert Strang, in fact, was one of those hardy human plants that can grow and flourish mentally and morally in any soil. He had been but a few years under the village teacher. The school in which he had learnt most was the world, where the lessons are undoubtedly very difficult, but, if once mastered, are most salutary. In the few books which he had, in the weekly sermons to which he listened, in the ever-varying shows of earth and sky, and in the rustic gatherings and merrymakings, he got abundant food both for mind and heart. Then, during the long quiet days when he was guiding the plough in the meadow, he found a favourite opportunity for thinking over what he had seen and read, and for forming his notions of men and things. In this way, he had made up his mind on most of the subjects that crop up in rural life, and was able to express his views, not only in the broad vernacular, but also, when occasion called, in good English. Altogether, he was a fair specimen of a man of Nature's own training, or what pious people used to call "one of God Almighty's own scholars."

"Don't you think I wad be richt, Gilbert Strang, to ceet him before the Presbytery, and if I canna get redress there to try the Law?"

"Ye wad be just playin' into his haunds, Mr Manson."

"In what way, Gilbert?"

"Ye wad mak him staund oot before the public as a martyr, and that's what a' thae kind want to be. What I would advise wad be, to gie him rope."

"What dae ye mean, Gilbert?"

"He kens the bothies only by hearsay; and he has spoken a lot o' nonsense aboot them. Let him alane. He'll gang deeper and deeper into the mess. Then he'll find himsel in a habble and be obleeged to apologeese."

"Apologeese!" cried Manson, "catch a minister apologeese! Dod man! they're never wrang. At the time o' the Reformation, they jist shifted the doctrine o' infallibility from the Pope's shouthers on to their ain; and now, instead o' ane, we hae thousands o' Popes."

"That may be," replied Strang, "only ca' canny. Look before ye loup. Mind the proverb, 'Haste maks waste.'"

"Dod that's true," replied Manson. "But eh man! I wad gie a gude roond sum to see the gabbie body obleeged to tak back and swallow a' the nonsense he's been talkin'."

"Weel!" said Gilbert, "ye'll soon see it."

Two days after this conversation on the road, winter weather had come, in all its severity. It was seven o'clock at night. Outside the farmhouse of Pitlour, the cold round moon looked down upon snow-clad roofs and stacks, icicles hanging from the eaves, the pump in the barnyard sheathed in straw, and the ploughs hard bound in the meadow by the frost. But inside in the bothy, which was attached to the house, all was bright and warm. A fire made of wood and coals blazed in the chimney; an old-fashioned oil lamp called a cruisie, hung from the mantelpiece; and the combined light of these two fell upon three well-fed, well-conditioned, rustic faces. On one side of the chimney was Gilbert Strang, deeply interested in the weekly newspaper; on the other side was his fellow-ploughman, Sandy Downie, laboriously scraping out of his fiddle the tune of "Auld Lang Syne"; and in front of the blaze was Jim Lochty, the cattle boy, with a copy of Burns in his hand, crooning over the words of a familiar song. In the background, two bedsteads made of rough wood, but with white pillows and sheets, looked snug and comfortable. The occupants were interrupted by a knock at the door, and who should walk in but the Rev. Jeremiah MacGuffog. He apologised for what might be called "a surprise visit." But he said he held the opinion that the minister was the friend of everyone in the parish, and that he should be able to drop in upon his parishioners unceremoniously at any time, and take them as he found them. Strang said that they were glad to see him, and asked him to take a seat.

Sitting down and scanning the place carefully, the minister said: "You heard from my sermon on Sabbath that I am deeply interested in the bothy question; and I want to be thoroughly acquainted with it."

Strang smiled and said to himself: "Jeddart Justice. He condemned and executed us on Sunday, and now he is going to try us."

"I must confess," said the minister, "that I am surprised to see your place look so tidy and comfortable. You heard, I suppose, that I was coming."

"No," said Strang. "The goodwife, Mrs Wedderspoon, looks upon this as part of her own house, and is just as particular about it as she is about the rooms where her two sons sleep. No place could be cleaner or more comfortable."

"But your food?" asked the minister. "Is it not rather coarse?"

"Well, sir!" replied Strang, "it would be coarse to the like of you. But for hard working, healthy, country folk, out in the open air, could anything be better than well-boiled porridge and sweet milk for breakfast and supper, and kail and meat and potatoes for dinner? And looking at us, you would say that our food agrees with us."

"Then," said the minister, after a thoughtful pause, "I am sorry to see that you have no means of improving your mind. You seem to have no books."

"Oh yes," said Strang, opening the door of a cupboard, "we have a few. Look! here are Brown's 'Dictionary of the Bible,' 'Shakespeare,' some of Sir Walter Scott's works; and Jim has 'Burns' in his hand. Anyone who masters all these is better educated than most people."

"I'm surprised," remarked the minister gravely, "that you read 'Burns.' He has some very objectionable passages."

"He's a mixture of good and bad," replied Strang, "just like every other author. If we read no author that is not absolutely pure, we shall read none at all. He's a poor creature that can't pick out the good and throw away the bad."

"I suppose," remarked the minister, "that there is a good deal of whisky consumed here sometimes?"

"For months," said Strang, "we never taste it."

"When you see," said the minister, "so many of your fellow-creatures abuse it, why not set them a good example and abstain from it altogether?"

"Well, sir," replied Strang, "I've thought of

that, and I have also thought that if I were to abstain from everything that is abused, I would soon, like the Irishman's horse, come to the last straw and die of starvation."

"Of course," said the minister "you have none of the salutary influences of a home?"

"Oh yes, sir," answered Strang, "we go down to the kitchen every night, and have a crack and snuff with the goodman, a gossip with the goodwife, and a game at 'catch the ten' with the sons, and finish up with family worship. To all intents and purposes we are members of the family."

"I am told," said the minister, "that there is a good deal of loose talk in bothies, and that one bad man often corrupts the whole lot."

"I fear, sir," replied Strang, "that that's the fault, not of bothies, but of human nature itself. In almost every company objectionable persons will be found. They are to be met with in the most select society, and even, I am told, in the rooms of divinity students. You'll correct me if I am wrong. There was Mr Joram's son of Kilbaigie, a divinity student, rusticated last year for being tipsy and uproarious at a gathering in his own lodgings."

Then after a little, Mr MacGuffog said—"this bothy of yours seems to be an exception. Is it not?"

"No," said Strang, "all in this neighbourhood are very much alike."

"Then I'm afraid," said the minister, looking very uncomfortable, "I've done the farmers injustice."

"Indeed you have, sir," replied Strang earnestly, "and they feel it very keenly. The country folk are talking of leaving your church in a body. 'Nurseries of hell' and 'servants of the devil' are uncommonly strong terms."

"But such terms," said the minister, "if I am rightly informed, must apply to the system as it exists elsewhere."

"Not so far as I am aware," said Strang. "Besides, your remarks referred to this neighbourhood."

Then after a long pause the minister said in a tone of great embarrassment, "What am I to do?"

"Well, sir," replied Strang, "I think you know better than I do. But what seems to me the only straightforward plan is this: if you have been wrong, confess it frankly. If you have done injustice to the people, apologise."

"Well," said the minister, "I shall first visit the other bothies in the parish, and I shall be guided by what I see there." Then after a pause he said—"But how do you account for the great outcry that has been raised against bothies?"

"Partly in this way, sir," said Strang. "There are some ministers (you will excuse me for saying it) that are like our sporting lairds. They must have the excitement of the chase. If they start a heresy case, that's their highest game and gives them their best sport. But not always lighting upon that, they have no difficulty in finding what they consider some social evil. Then they give the view halloo, and are after it in full cry through thick and thin."

"Ah!" said the minister, rising, "you are hard upon us poor clergy; but there may be a little truth in what you say. Good night." And away he went.

Next Sunday morning there was a great gathering of country folk at the church. They were discussing the rumour, that the minister was going to apologise. Some believed it, while others thought that it was too good to be true. Among the latter was old Manson.

"Apologeese," he sneered, "no, no. A black

coat never surrenders. When he has been steekit in by the bethal, he can say what he likes, and no' ane daur utter a cheep. Na, na, the poopit has been ower lang the seat o' an oracle. It's no' gaun to become the stule o' repentance."

But old Manson was wrong. Towards the end of the sermon, which was on the text, " Bear ye one another's burdens," the minister came to a dead pause. There was a terrible stillness all over the church. Every ear was on the alert to catch what was coming, and nervous people held down their heads. Then the minister, looking ghastly pale, and speaking with slow deliberation, said :

"Brethren, my great desire is to find out what your burdens are, and to help you to bear them ; but last Sabbath I must admit that I failed. I had always heard that the Bothy System was one of the curses of this country; and I had never heard a word said in its defence. Very naturally, in calling upon the people of this neighbourhood to put away the evil thing from among them, I used very strong language. Brethren, I have since discovered that, as far as this parish is concerned, I was wrong; and I now apologise to the farming people in particular and the congregation in general. May this be a warning to us all—to you as well as me—not to be too hasty in forming judgments regarding our fellow-creatures."

Here was an event altogether unprecedented! No one had ever heard of a minister confessing from the pulpit that he had made a mistake. It was the result of the purest Christian candour; but had it proceeded from policy it would have been a master-stroke. With one sentence the minister turned the hearts of the people from the fiercest indignation right round to an enthusiastic love. The women-folk especially were loud in his praises.

"Oh!" they exclaimed, "wasn't it like a real Christian to own that he was wrang; and didn't he look rale bonny when he was daein' it?" And they all agreed that it was Gilbert Strang, who by his wonderful cleverness had opened the minister's eyes, and made him see that it was his duty to confess.

On the Monday afterwards, Gilbert was ploughing the Five-Acre Lea. To one fond of rustic associations it was a pleasant picture; the pair of horses sleek and well-fed, bending their heads over their strong chests, lifting their legs leisurely and together, and pulling the plough slowly through the stiff loam; the knife-like coulter evenly cutting a narrow strip of the green turf; the shining share turning it over and forming another long ridge of fresh earth; the man holding steadily the plough-tails and looking contented and happy; and over all, the sombre sky of a winter afternoon gradually darkening towards the dusk. As he was turning the plough at the headrig, he heard himself hailed in a cheery voice. He looked round, and there was Manson of the Hole, with his face in a broad grin of delight.

Shaking the ploughman's hand, and then slapping him vehemently on the shoulder, he roared out, "Eh, man, ye're an awfu' billy. This is an age o' novelties, and ye've brocht aboot ane o' the greatest o' them a'. A minister standin' in the poopit and confessin' to his folk that he had been wrang! Wha ever heard the like? It's an event in the history o' the kirk. And the man that had the head and the tongue to manage a' this — here he is, wastin' himsel on wark that the stupidest clod-happer could dae. By the Lord Hairy! it's no' richt! You should hae been a minister yersel, settin' them a lesson o' straightforwardness; and as sure as I am a livin' sinner they require it. Man! I'll tell ye what I'll dae. I'm no' a rich man, but I'll lend ye twa hunder pounds to gang to the college; and ye can pay it back whenever it suits ye. Ye needna hurry."

Strang was taken aback; and for about a minute was silent, fascinated evidently by the prospect which had thus suddenly been called up before him. At last he said:

"Mr Manson! dae ye really mean that? It's awfu' generous; and I'm half inclined to tak yer offer. But no, the kirk is no' my trade; the harness wadna sit easy. Nor yet the schule; my nerves wadna stand a' the tear and wear that's required to stir up a' kinds o' young brains. Besides, I canna gie up an open air country life. It has nearly a' the advantages I care aboot. We get the great natural medicines —fresh air, sunlight, pure water, perfect quiet, and sound sleep. We hae the best food; for what could be mair nourishin' than milk, eggs, and oatmeal, all fresh and unadulterated? And we hae the best opportunities (if we only hae the gumption to tak them) of improvin' oor minds, for we live in the workshop o' nature, and see the coontless wonders which she is producin' a' the year roond."

"But dae ye no' think it richt," asked Manson, "to raise yersel as sae mony hae dune, to a higher position in society?"

"Weel," replied Strang slowly, "I'm no' jist sure aboot that. It seems to me a kind o' selfishness. Should we no' think o' raisin' others? We owe a duty to oorsels, nae doot, but also to those wha hae produced us and brocht us up. That's the true way in which the masses are to be raised—not by being patronised by their superiors, but by being led onwards and upwards by men of their own class. Not that I think I could ever lead them; but I could assist them that are really able to lead them."

"Weel," said Manson, going away, "my offer is still afore ye, whenever ye like to tak it."

Year after year passed away, and Gilbert Strang continued most religiously to save every penny that he could. When his hoardings amounted to a handsome sum, he looked for some way of laying them out at interest. Now, there was in Mr MacGuffog's congregation a Mr Melville, a lawyer and banker of unquestionable respectability, a prominent elder in the kirk, and the brother of a celebrated D.D. To many of the church members he had become the guide, philosopher, and friend. Besides giving them his advice, he took charge of their spare cash and got an investment for it. To this gentleman Strang had no hesitation in committing his hard-earned money, with the injunction, that the interest when it fell due was to be added to the principal, and the aggregate sum in this way allowed to accumulate. At the end of five years, his affairs had prospered so well that he saw a prospect of buying back his inheritance. He would borrow a sum from Manson, giving him in return a bond upon the property; and that sum added to his savings would make up the purchase money. He had got Manson's hearty consent, he had instructed Mr Melville to realise his investments, and he had written to his mother to tell her the joyful tidings, and to say that he would be over at her house on Saturday evening to discuss the whole matter.

It was a beautiful day at the end of June, and Strang was busy among the haymakers in the Bog. The occasion was important; and all the inmates of the farm—master and servants, old and young, men and women, and even the dogs—were engaged. Amidst a perpetual ripple of gossip, joke, and laughter, they merrily turned over the tanned grass, put it up in cocks (or, as it was called in that district, *coles*), and carefully raking the cleared space, made the field look tidy and fresh. The sight of the abundant and well-conditioned crop; the delightful scent that arose from it; the twitter of the swallows that wheeled around; and above all the glorious weather, exhilarated every soul. And when the cart, driven by Jim Lochty and containing the dinner, appeared at the gate of the field, they laughed aloud in their joy; for what can be more delightful to a hungry human creature than the prospect of being seated on a heap of fragrant hay with a large *bap* in one hand and a tankard of nut-brown ale in the other. But what was the matter with Jim? He was all excitement. He had evidently something startling to tell; and, like your ordinary bearer of sensational news, even when it is bad, he had a sort of grim pleasure in delivering it. Before he came up he cried out:—

"Gilbert Strang, yer banker, Mr Melville, has cut his throat and has left a letter to say that he has made awa wi' a' the folks' siller."

Strang was stunned, and for some time could do nothing but stare at Jim, wondering if he were telling the truth.

At last he said: "I don't believe it. Mr Melville o' a' folk! Somebody has been hoaxing ye."

"Na," said Jim, "it's perfectly true. It was the polisman that tellt me; and he had seen him quite stiff and had read the letter. A' the folk were talkin' aboot it. Look! there's Mr Proud o' the Hill passin'. Gang and speir at him."

Mr Proud had stopped his gig and was beckoning to Strang; and when Strang went over to him, it was only to hear a confirmation of the terrible report. But that was not all. Misfortune seems to take a savage delight not only in knocking her victim down, but in trampling upon him after he is down. Mr Proud had another sad calamity to tell, namely, that Mr Manson had been found that morning dead in bed.

Here was the end of all Strang's labour. This double loss dispelled at once the dream which had lighted up all his future — the hope of regaining the inheritance of his ancestors, that white two-storeyed house, with the sunny garden in front, and the snug farm buildings behind, on whose walls the history of the family seemed to be written, and where the associations of his own happy boyhood, like the bright and fresh dewdrops of a summer morning, hung upon every bush and tree. A cloud of despondency fell upon him; and, seen through it, the sunny landscape and the merry faces of the haymakers seemed incongruous and almost unbearable.

His spirit, however, was too robust to be long weighed down. Towards evening he threw off his load, and asked himself if he had, on the whole, any good reason for complaining? He had, indeed, lost the opportunity of realising a happiness which was chiefly made up of sentiment; but, on the other hand, what blessings were still spared to him? Health, strength, congenial employment, wholesome food, sound sleep, fresh air, the glories of the universe, appreciative friends, and a kind Providence. He who could mope and mourn in the face of all these advantages was not a man at all, but a cowardly cur.

Then the thought of his mother arose in his mind. How would she bear it? Beneath the double blow of her husband's bankruptcy and death, the poor body's courage had given way. Thoroughly demoralised, she considered herself a victim, and expected restitution, not only from her friends and the public at large, but even from Providence. She had, therefore, staked her whole happiness upon the recovery of the pleasant steading and fields at Sunnybrae. And now that the recovery was impossible, most bitter would be her disappointment, and endless would be her grumbling against society at large and even against Providence.

Strang's mother lived at Cauldale, a solitary place four miles north of Pitlour. It stood far apart from other dwellings, on the side of an uncultivated hill. It had once been a row of thatched cottages; but with the exception of the one at the east end, they had been allowed to fall into decay, and now stood roofless and empty. The hearths which had once been lit up by warm household fires, and the still warmer smiles of family affection, were now covered with rubbish and overgrown with weeds. In the one which was still habitable, Mrs Strang had been allowed by the Laird to take up her abode; and by the aid of her son and some kind friends she had managed to get the means of making a scanty living. A cow grazing on the braes, a pig fed on the refuse of the garden, a row of bee-hives and a flock of poultry, gave her a supply of milk, butter, cheese, pork, honey, and eggs — part of which she devoted to her own use, but the most of which she carried into the nearest town and sold for hard cash. She even utilised the crops that grew beyond the range of cultivation. In early summer she culled the young nettles to make *kail*. In autumn she gathered the brambleberries to make jam for her afternoon tea; and a bed of wormwood growing on the hillside in front of her house supplied her with all the medicine she ever took.

On the Saturday evening when she expected her son's visit, she was seated with her knitting on a chair in front of her cottage. She was in high spirits, and anticipated with great pleasure the discussing with Gilbert all the details of taking possession of Sunnybrae. Soon she saw him in the distance coming striding through the pasture land. Still working at her stocking, she went down the face of the hill to meet him. But when he drew near, instead of that jubilant smile which she had expected to see on his face, there was a look of depression.

"Gilbert," she exclaimed, "what's wrang? Something has happened. Ye canna hide it from yer mither. Tell me at ance."

He told her; and with a cry of lamentation she dropped on the ground and sat there, wringing her hands and bemoaning her fate: "what hae I dune, what hae I dune, to be afflickit in this way — blow after blow — blow after blow — and after slavin' and starvin' and savin'. But that man (what's his name?) canna hae swallowed the siller. He maun hae spent it on some folk. They should be socht oot and made to pay it back."

Strang thought it best not to answer his mother, but to allow her to give vent to her feelings. Then raising her gently up, taking her by the arm, and telling her that she must come and give him a cup of tea, as he was ready to faint, he led her into her cottage. It was a poor place, but the care which had been taken to make it comfortable in honour of his coming touched his heart. A clear fire was burning behind the two iron bars that served for a grate. The cracked hearthstone and rough earthen floor had been swept and whitened. The most was made of the scanty bits of furniture, the wreck of her former household; and everything was clean and in its proper place. A snowy cloth covered the frail round table; the marriage china was arranged in order; his favourite brambleberry jam was in a glass dish; his favourite buttered toast simmered before the fire; and the only armchair in the house was placed for him in his favourite chimney-corner.

Wiping her eyes occasionally, and moaning "Oh dear," she poured out a cup of tea for him; but refused to take any herself, and sat rocking herself to and fro. Then came another outburst, "Why did ye ever trust that man? I'm sure I tellt ye weel aboot 'im."

"Mother, mother," he said in a deprecating tone, "hoo can ye say so? Ye never did."

"That I did," she moaned out. "But ye never listen to what I say. Nae wonder ye forget."

Strang saw that reasoning would do no good; and so he sat silent while she continued to give vent to her feelings. And to his great relief, a knock came to the door, and a gentleman, well-dressed and well-mannered, entered.

"Mr Strang, I presume," he said. "I must

beg your pardon for intruding. I called at Pitlour, and they sent me on here."

Catching fresh alarm, and seeing in this visit a continuation of the coil of troubles in which they had got involved, the mother cried out, "Oh sir! what are ye gaun to dae wi' 'im?"

The gentleman, with a kindly smile, said, "There's nothing to cause alarm; quite the reverse. I am Mr Kemp, Mr Manson's lawyer."

And then in a calm manner, as if it was the sort of thing that occurred every day, he told that Mr Manson had left his money and other belongings to Gilbert Strang.

Mrs Strang burst into a rapture of delight: "Eh, dae ye hear that! It's an answer to my prayers. I aye said that Providence wad mak up to us what He had made us suffer."

But Strang himself was strangely silent. At length he said, "I don't see how I can take it, sir."

"No' tak it!" screamed his mother. "Are ye mad?"

"No, mother!" said Strang, quietly, "this money should have been given to Mr Manson's relatives."

"He has got no relatives," said Mr Kemp, "and he expressly says that he leaves it to you as the man whom he most respects, and who will "guide the money best"; and if you don't take it, why, it must go to the Queen; and in the ocean of her wealth it will be a mere drop, and will do good to nobody."

"Dae ye hear that!" said the mother. "The Queen indeed; set her up! She's got ower muckle already. She would tak everything."

"Then," said Gilbert, "if I maun tak it, I canna spend it on mysel. I'll pay my father's debts, and wipe off the family disgrace."

"Gilbert Strang!" said his mother, "are ye mad? Sir! ye'll no' allow him to dae this. The money wasna left for this."

"Mother," he said, quietly, "my father's memory is ane o' oor dearest possessions. There's a blot on it, the blot o' bankruptcy. I want to rub that aff, so that you and me may hae nae cause to blush when his name is mentioned."

Utterly foiled, the poor woman collapsed, saying in a tone of resignation, "Weel, weel, gang yer ain gait, and leave me here to slave, and starve, and dee. Ye'll maybe wipe yer faither's debts aff yer conscience, but ye'll sune hae yer mither's death in their place."

Gilbert now rose to go back with Mr Kemp. His mother refused to shake hands with him;

but he clapped her on the back, and said, "Courage, mother! there may be some siller left, after payin' a' the debts, to buy Sunnybrae yet."

When they were outside, Mr Kemp said, "if you carry out this Quixotic plan of yours, you'll have nothing left."

"I can't help that," returned Strang; "I must do what's right."

Strang lost no time in carrying out his resolve. Ere a few weeks had passed, his father's creditors, very much to their astonishment, were paid the full amount of what was owing them, along with interest. On the next Sunday morning, as he put on his old and faithful Sunday clothes, he felt a satisfaction which he had never experienced before. The stain on his father's memory—a memory otherwise bright—was removed, and he almost felt that his deceased parent was near, smiling approval of what had been done.

His appearance among the loungers at the church door created quite a stir. Every eye was upon him. The farmers and their wives pressed forward to shake him cordially by the hand. They said nothing, for their limited vocabulary contained no form of words suitable for such an extraordinary occasion; but their looks expressed their feelings. Though they would not very likely, if placed in his circumstances, have done what he had done; yet they could not help admiring him. As he stood before them in his well-worn attire, he looked like a hero of the antique type; and the patches on his coat appeared more than ever like badges of honour.

Meanwhile his mother, on the lonely slopes of Cauldale, moped and grumbled. She felt herself a poor, forlorn wretch, deserted not only by her son but by Providence also; and she took a morbid pleasure in thinking that no one had ever been so ill used as she. But one afternoon, as she sat at her solitary "four-hours," her son burst in, with every feature beaming. She was then quite prepared for the good news that he brought. The creditors were so delighted with his unexpected conduct, that they had met and agreed to return to him half the money. With that, and the remainder of Manson's legacy, he had bought back Sunnybrae.

"So by next Martinmas," he said, "ye'll be in yer ain auld house, mither."

Bright glowed the ben-end, or parlour, of Sunnybrae on the evening of the 12th November.

Bright, also, were the occupants, Gilbert Strang and his mother. They had come in on the forenoon of the 11th, and had been hard at work "pittin' things to richts." Mrs Strang had complained bitterly about the state in which everything had been left; but she had at last arranged things so that they could now sit down with some degree of comfort.

"Looking round," she said, "on a' the auld things in their auld places, I feel as if I had been dreamin' aboot livin' in a strange country, and that I had waukened up to find mysel at hame. There is only ae great want,—the presence o' yer faither. But I canna help thinkin' that he is here in spirit, and shares in our joy. And oh, Gilbert! glad he maun be that a' his debts are paid, and that naebody can say that they hae lost onything by him. You were richt, and I was wrang."

THE GENTLEMAN TRAMP.

JOHN FAIRGRIEVE, better known as Hillend, the name of his farm, had been born with a strong appetite for knowledge. Had his education been attended to in his youth, he would very likely have been a great reader. But as he had never got into the way of using books with facility, he was driven to seek his mental food in the actual world around him; and this he did with the greatest assiduity. In plain language, he was a notorious newsmonger, a collector of all the "clashes" of the neighbourhood. In bright summer weather, before the hay harvest came on, and when "there was naething pushin'," it was his delight to stand at his farm gate, under the large plane tree, with his snuff-box in his hand, and exchange news with all the passers-by. It did not matter who they were. The farmer in his gig, the ploughman on his cart, the baker driving his van, the beggarwife with her brats and her wallets, were all obliged to "stand and deliver." In fact, Hillend was a sort of informal turnpike man, levying mental toll on the king's highway.

Very like him in this inveterate love for tittle-tattle were his two sisters, Lizzie and Grizzie, who kept house for him. They were seldom seen separate. They hunted in couples. And their prey was generally some country laddie that came into the farmyard for milk or butter. They took complete possession of the unlucky urchin. He had no more chance of escape than a gooseberry which has fallen before two greedy hens. The one examined him, and then the other cross-examined him, or (to use the old Scotch phraseology) the one speired and the other back-speired, until the poor child was turned inside out, or, as Geordie Faw, the cattleman, expressed it, "fairly flypeit."

It was eight o'clock on a wild October night. Outside, in the farmyard, were darkness and a fierce gale that rattled at the windows and howled at the chimney tops, and swirled round the stacks and into every hole and corner. Inside, in the farm kitchen, were light and warmth and bright dishes on the walls, and still brighter faces grouped round the blazing fire. With the exception of Collie the dog and Mottie the cat, all were busy in their own different ways. Miss Lizzie was at the churn, and Miss Grizzie at the spinning-wheel. Willie Foster and Pate Mackie, the two ploughmen, were playing at draughts, or, as they called it, "the dam-brod." Geordie Faw was cobbling his shoes. The itinerant tailor, John Glen, seated cross-legged on a chair, was mending the farmer's coat. And Hillend himself, what was he doing? Occupying the place of honour at the left side of the fire, and, with the usual snuff-box in his hand, he was keeping up the conversation, or, in other words, "ca'in the crack." As the corn and the potatoes were safely gathered in, he was in capital spirits, and bent upon making both himself and the others happy.

You would have thought that there was very little entertainment to be got in that quiet homely scene; but you would have been mistaken. First of all, there was Glen, the tailor, with a tongue as sharp and slick as his own shears, and with odds and ends of scandal as many and varied as his own clippings. Then in came Sandy Livingstone, fresh from a visit to the smithy, and bursting with all the "clavers" of the parish—who was dead, who was going to be married, who had *failed*, who had been fou last July fair, who had been up before the Session, how Grangemire Mary had got her leave, and Geordie Clephane had lost his watch at Kirkcaldy market. And while they were still enjoying these tit-bits, and rolling them like sweet morsels under their tongue, who should appear but a mysterious stranger, foot-sore and tired with travel. All grew quiet to look at him. This was no ordinary tramp.

His clothes were fashionably cut, though threadbare and soiled; and his features and hands were thin and delicate, though tanned by the weather. The company were prepared to hear that he had once seen better days; but they broke into a murmur of astonishment when he told them that he had been an Oxford man and a man about town, and that he had tramped all the way from London. "An Oxford swell!" "A London man!" "Tramped all the way!" Hillend's face glowed with the anticipation of hearing a wonderful story, and in his excitement he took four or five *snuffs* consecutively. Miss Lizzie and Miss Grizzie stopped their work, rose to their feet, drew near to the stranger, devouring him with their eyes, and eager to "speir and back-speir." They, indeed, set him down to a supper of bread and cheese and milk; but they began at the same time to question him about himself and his adventures. However, he said that if they would kindly wait till he had refreshed and strengthened himself with the meal they had placed before him, he would give them a full and true account of his strange career. They were therefore obliged, meanwhile, to satisfy their curiosity by watching him while he stowed away the viands with wonderful celerity. At length his ravenous appetite was appeased; and, wiping his mouth with his coat sleeve, and begging pardon for doing so, and giving as an excuse that he hadn't a pocket-handkerchief, he began the story of his adventures. In after days it was often repeated, first by himself and then by others, so that I am able to give it for the most part in his own words.

"My father was rich, but I am almost ashamed to confess that he did not make his money in a very nice way. He was, you see, a pawnbroker in the High Street of Edinburgh. When I was a boy I used often to be in the shop on a

Saturday night, and, upon my soul, I used to pity the poor quivering wretches that came in, raising money on their furniture, their very bed, and even the family Bible. I have seen a poor woman, half-stripped herself, take off the clothes from a puny child in her arms, and pawn them. All kinds of scenes went on, haggling and arguing, and cursing and swearing. The words of one customer, especially, I can never forget. He was a broken-down author, puffy and shaky. He was angry because he had not got enough upon his silver watch.

"'You cursed old Jew,' he said to my father, 'I'll tell you what you are. You're a wrecker. You wait for those who are cast ashore by the waves of misfortune, and rob them of the remnants of their property.'

"'No, no,' said my father, 'I accommodate them with money to keep them alive, and in return take only the things they can spare.'

"My father himself did not like the trade, for he gave it up, and went to live in a villa at Eskbank. He continued, however, to lend money in private; but it was on a large scale. Young gentlemen, regular swells, used to call at the house and be closeted with him, and had difficulty in coming to an agreement. I heard one say as he was leaving, 'one hundred per cent. is tremendous.' 'So is the risk,' was all my father's answer.

"My mother was of an easy-going disposition, had no head for figures, and left the management of all money matters to her husband. Her whole care was devoted to me, her only child. I was the apple of her eye. Dear old mother! how I wish that I had appreciated her more!

"As we sat at the fire on a winter evening, she would say, 'Ben! my lad, we must give you the best education. I would like to see you a gentleman before I die.'

"'Nonsense!' my father would say, 'I'll not waste any money upon Latin and Greek, and rubbish of that kind. The training I got will be good enough for him.'

"However, to our great astonishment, he came round to mother's view. You see, he intended that I should carry on the money-lending business, and he thought that if I were sent to a high-class school, I would form a wide connection among young aristocratic spendthrifts, which would be of great service to me. So the question came to be discussed, 'to what school should I be sent?' and to settle this question our next door neighbour assisted us.

"This man was Captain Beaumont, but was popularly called 'the Earl.' He was, as he told everybody, 'a real gentleman that had taken a thousand years to be produced, not a shoddy one that can be turned out nowadays in a few weeks.' He was tall, grey, and scraggy, with a backbone as stiff as a walking-stick, and with a head that was uncommonly small, but that was 'large enough,' as our minister remarked, 'for all the ideas he had got to put into it.' His house was, like himself, cheerless but pretentious. He called it Dunmore, which, you must know, was the name of the castle where his ancestors had lived, heaven knows how long ago. He had a doited old serving-man, who was dressed in the family livery, and waited at table, and served the thin broth and scraggy mutton on the family silver. There was also above the dining-room mantelpiece his genea-logical tree, with many branches and leaves, and each leaf had on it the name of one of his fore-fathers, and on the topmost leaf was written his own name, 'Reginald Algernon Beaumont, the present earl.'

"For some time the Earl was very haughty

towards us, throwing us a word occasionally, just as he would throw it to a neighbour's dog. But by and by he made an excuse for calling on us; and in a few weeks he came in regularly every night to have a game of draughts at our fireside. 'His hungry nose,' my father said, 'had scented the havannas and the Glenlivet.' In the first part of the evening he was silent and grumpy, as if he looked down upon our society, and was half angry with himself for being in it. But when the whisky and cigars were placed on the table, he brightened up and grew pleasant and sociable, and would talk for hours about his ancestors, and would tell that he was the lineal descendant of Reginald de Beaumont, who came into Scotland in the reign of David the First, and that he was, therefore, the Earl of Abernethy; and then he would blackguard the House of Lords for not acknowledging his title, and would call them 'Brummagem peers, mostly made out of lucky lawyers, brewers, and cotton-spinners.' On one of these occasions, my mother took courage to talk about me, saying that she wished to make me a gentleman, and asked his advice as to what should be done. He was startled, and, screwing up his nose, said :—

"'My dear Madam, you can't make your son a gentleman. You can't put blue blood into his veins and give him a pedigree a thousand years long. But you may give him a gentlemanly education, and make him as good a gentleman as ninety-nine out of every hundred who assume the name. Send him to a high-class English school and then to Oxford. There he will get up the classics, the only branch worthy of a gentleman.'

"So by the Earl's advice I was sent to Vere de Vere College, in Yorkshire: Principal, the Rev. Augustus Caesar, LL.D. The doctor, as he was called, received me in a very friendly manner. So did the pupils, after their own way; rather a rollicking kind of way, however. They were healthy, riotous, and as full of mischief as monkeys. Surrounding me, staring at me, and pulling me about, they plied me with all sorts of questions — what was my governor? had he lots of tin? was Scotland such a wild place? how did I feel in trousers? had I brought my kilt with me? Then they began 'to make me at home,' as they called it. One borrowed a sixpence from me; another, learning that I could not box, showed me the way and gave me a bloody nose; and all of them joined in crying out, that, as a new boy, I must pay my footing and stand them a jolly spread of pies and tarts and rum-shrub.

"For the first few days I had rather a lively time. As I was a new boy, they thought it only right to practise all their tricks upon me, such as putting a bunch of thistles in my bed, filling my boots with hot water, and putting cobbler's wax upon my seat, which held me fast when the doctor called me to get up. They also exercised their ingenuity in inventing nicknames for me, and I was addressed as 'Scotty,' 'Haggis,' 'Jew,' and 'Balls' (for they had ferreted out that my father had been a pawnbroker). But at length Lord Gulpington, who was the trump card of the college, being the heir to a marquisate, claimed me as his fag, and would allow no one to torment me except himself. He slept in the same room with me, and generally awoke me in the morning by throwing his slipper at my head. Then I got up, and, after dressing hurriedly, went down for his boots and his hot water. During the day I did anything that he required, and at night I often had to smuggle in 'grub and lush,' as he called it. We got on well together. I was quite delighted to be connected in any way with a lord; and after a while he said that next to his bull dog, Griffin, which he kept at the butcher's in the village, he liked me best of any creature about the place.

"As far as the body was concerned, the pupils got on very well. They had capital appetites, which they constantly attended to; and they were not content with the abundance that was placed before them, but they were constantly devouring apples, oranges, hardbake, and gingerbeer. Most hearty were they also in taking physical exercise. They played cricket and football, and talked about them incessantly, as if they had been the chief end of man; and they ran at hounds and hares as if they had been hunting a fortune, and not a dirty little boy with a bag of paper scraps.

"The physical training, indeed, was splendid, but I can't say as much for the mental training. With the exception of a little Greek, the thing that we always seemed to be grinding at was Latin. Our grammar book was in Latin. Our reading book was in Latin. The very grace said at table was in Latin. I tried to fix Latin in my head, but it came out again as fast as I put it in. They endeavoured to improve my memory by giving me several hundred verses to commit, but that only made me worse. In despair, one day I told the doctor that I would never be able to learn Latin. He told me that I must learn it, if I wished to be educated. I then had the presumption to ask him what was the use of it.

"'Oh,' he said, 'it is the best instrument for training the faculties. Besides, it is the "open sesame" into good society.'

"Had I been the only backward pupil, I might have thought that the fault lay in my stupidity. But with the exception of two or three, the other pupils were nearly as bad as myself, and detested their lessons. If a knowledge of Latin was to be the 'open sesame' into good society, I'm afraid they would never get in.

"At the end of four years my course at school was finished; and before proceeding to Oxford I spent a few weeks at home. One evening my father, in his business-like way, asked me to make up an account of the items I had got in return for the money he had laid out,—in other words, to tell him distinctly how much I had learnt.

"Afraid to go into details, I said, 'Well, at least, I've learnt the ways and manners of a gentleman.'

"'Ah,' replied my father, 'to be sure, that's worth all the book knowledge. You'll be better able to do business with gentlemen.'

"In this way I had staved off an ugly question; but in my own room, before going to bed that night, I ran over in my mind what I had learnt and what I had not learnt at school. I had learnt to play cricket and football, to run, to leap, to box, to smoke, to drink beer, and make bets. I had *not* learnt to write a good hand, to spell correctly, to count correctly, and to know something of the history and geography of my native country.

"My mother came to have some notion of the true state of matters. She had asked me to write to the minister, inviting him to our house on a certain night to meet some friends, and unfortunately I had spelt *meet* with an *a*. The minister was a great humorist, and this was an occasion for a joke which he could not neglect. Consequently, he called next morning, with my letter in his hand, to ask what kind of meat he would bring — beef, or mutton, or pork. My mother, when she understood the mistake, felt it keenly. So, one evening at the fireside, while the Earl and my father were having their game of draughts, she said:

"'Well, Ben, I hope you will get on at Oxford, and correct all your deficiencies, and come out a perfect scholar.'

"'My dear madam,' said the Earl, 'if any place can make him a scholar Oxford is that place. It has got all the means; it has the most money, the best teachers, and the greatest reputation.'

"My mother, however, although she knew it not, was cruelly deceived. To men who were in love with learning, Oxford gave every facility for maturing their scholarship. But to those who had no such love she could do nothing. Into this latter class I was unfortunate enough to fall. Lord Gulpington was there before me, and introduced me to his set, which consisted of the sons of the aristocratic and the wealthy. These youths, though passing through the curriculum of the University, were students merely in name. They did almost everything but study. Bless you! how could you expect them to do otherwise? What charms could they find in musty, out-of-date Latin and Greek works? They were young, healthy, spirited, and rich; and the bright and breathing world lay around them. Everything within them and without them called upon them to enjoy themselves. They, indeed, went through the farce of attending chapel in the morning, and lectures in the forenoon. But everyone, their teachers as well as themselves, knew it to be a farce. As soon as they went back to their rooms, they tossed their gowns aside, donned their sporting habiliments, and were off to the river, or the road, or the hunting-field, or the racecourse. Then back they came in the evening with a keen relish for other kinds of enjoyment. They feasted, they caroused, they gamboled, they sang jovial glees and choruses, and in fact rattled on as if life were to be a perpetual feast, without any such thing as duty, or trial, or suffering. In all these frolics I mingled. The jolly fellows, though they knew my origin, and called me by no other name than 'Balls,' were free and easy with me, played practical jokes upon me, borrowed my money, smoked my cigars, drank my wine, and even used my rooms for their parties.

"But all things come to an end; and the time arrived when the most of these devotees of pleasure had to lay aside their frivolities, and, in order to please the old folks at home, had to go in for their degree, or, as they called it, 'their smalls.' Many of them were, as it is called, 'plucked,' and no wonder! Their feathers were not home-grown, but were borrowed plumes stuck on with infinite labour and skill by tutors, and, therefore, came off easily. On me they would not even stick, and so I could not go up for the degree, and had not even the honour of being plucked.

"My poor parents were spared the chagrin of seeing the failure of their efforts to make me a gentleman. Before my Oxford career was finished, they died, both in the same week, the victims of the terrible Asiatic cholera, during its first visit to this country in 1832. As I now came into a considerable fortune, I saw no necessity for adopting a profession, or doing any useful work. To enjoy myself was, I thought, to be my only business; and the proper place for enjoyment was London, the centre of all that is pleasant and grand. So, as soon as I had wound up affairs in Edinburgh, I hastened to the metropolis.

"I put up at the Golden Cross, and proceeded, as it is called, 'to do the sights of London.' I visited picture galleries, museums, theatres, concert rooms, until I was tired out and disgusted. Then came on the most terrible feeling I ever experienced, a feeling which you busy and healthy people never had. *I did not know what to do.* I did not care to stroll about the streets, for the everlasting din and endless throng grew intolerable. I could not sit all day in the coffee-room of the hotel, staring at everyone that entered, and pretending to read the newspaper. When I got up in the morning, it seemed as if I would never manage to get through the day. Time was my great enemy. It loaded the present, and blocked up the future. How was I to kill it? To do this I would have been inclined to try almost anything. I now understood how men committed suicide through sheer weariness. I also felt the truth of the saying that idleness is the cause of nearly every crime, and that the idle man does not wait to be tempted, but of his own accord tempts the devil. My devil soon appeared.

"I had noticed among the inmates of the hotel a middle-aged, stout, and grey-headed gentleman, whom the waiters addressed as Colonel. He seemed to me to be round and oily with health, good nature, and jollity. One day, when he appeared to be idle, he sat down and had a talk with me. Without telling me much about himself, except that he been an officer in the Spanish service, he managed to extract from me a good deal about myself; and when he heard me complain about feeling dull, he at once placed his services at my disposal.

"'London dull!' he said, 'why, it's a paradise, a garden full of flowers, and I, like a bee, or rather a bumble-bee, have visited all of them.'

"And certainly no idle man could have a pleasanter companion than the Colonel. He was stimulating and enlivening, like the morning sunshine. His animal spirits and relish for life never flagged, and he was always ready, when the occasion turned up, to joke, to laugh, to eat, or to drink. Every day he had some novelty to offer. 'Now,' he would say, 'I'll give you a treat that you never had before;' and then he would drive me to a racecourse or some other resort of fashion, or he would take me to some famous old chop-house in the recesses of the city, or some new and gorgeous hotel in one of the fashionable thoroughfares; and, while we sat down to what he called, 'a nice little dinner,' he would introduce some new dish, or some new blend of whisky, or some new brand of wine; and while we discussed it he would smack his lips, rub his hands, and look at me as much as to say, 'Did I not tell you so?' His enjoyment of the pleasures of the great city never seemed to fail. The only thing, in fact, that ever failed with him was money. He sometimes had no change, or had forgotten his purse; but I was only too glad to pay his expenses in return for his company. I could not do without him. He had made life like a dream, a little feverish perhaps, but exceedingly pleasant.

"One night after the theatre, he took me to a house in the Haymarket, where, he said, we could sup cosily together. As soon as we had entered, to his great surprise, he found two old friends who had just arrived from the Continent. They were middle-aged, fashionably dressed, and well-mannered, and were introduced to me as Captain Spurr and Count Lago. At my invitation they joined us in a private room, where we supped on lobster and champagne, and all grew as sociable and as pleasant as you like. A game of whist was proposed, and the Colonel and I played against the other two for small stakes. We had astonishing luck, and won game after game;

and at the end of several hours, rose the winners of a considerable sum of money. Of course, we continued the practice of meeting and playing there, and night after night the same results happened. The Colonel and I always won. Such a thing had never been known before. They all attributed it to me; and even the landlord and the waiters complimented me, and wondered that I did not back my luck sufficiently. This was pleasant so far; but I did not like the idea of winning so much money, and feared that we might completely clean out our opponents, and I frankly told the Colonel my feelings on the matter, and suggested that we should stop.

"'Stop!' he exclaimed, 'we can't stop; we must give them their revenge. Oh, don't be afraid that you'll beggar them; they have plenty of the needful.'

"So on we drove in our career of victory, until our winnings amounted to a large sum. Then fortune changed, and, strange to say, went on as steadily against us as it had done for us, until our opponents had not only regained all they had lost, but had won some of our money.

"While on our way home that night I said

to the Colonel—'As our opponents have recouped themselves, we must now stop.'

"'Hang it!' said the Colonel, 'not just yet if you please. I can't afford to lose any money if you can. Let us adopt this method. We are so much money out of pocket. On our first game to-night, let us stake the double of that. If we lose, let us double it again; and let us go on doing this; and whenever the luck turns, and, hang it! you know, it must turn very soon, we shall, at one go, have won all our money back, and then we can cry quits.'

"This seemed a dangerous plan, but I felt that we must follow it. So on we went, night after night losing our games, and always piling up the money, till the stake had become something tremendous, and I became almost mad with excitement. To provide funds, I kept selling out my investments and lodging the money in a London bank; and to keep up my nerve I drank champagne incessantly — and then the crash came!

"I woke up one day with a head a mass of pain, a mouth as dry as a lime-kiln, and a confused memory of exciting scenes, to find myself in a bed in our nightly resort. On summoning the waiter, I learnt from him that I had been very tipsy, and that the Colonel and his friends had had some difficulty in managing me, and getting me to bed. I lost no time in going to the Golden Cross Hotel to see the Colonel, but to my horror I was told that the Colonel had left that morning with all his luggage. I understood now the hellish plot which had been devised for my ruin; but I thanked God that I had still ten thousand pounds in the bank. I hurried to the bank to make sure; but there I was met with the intelligence that a gentleman, that morning, had presented my cheque for the whole amount, and that all my money had been paid to him. I asked to see the cheque, thinking that it must have been forged; but no, there was my undoubted signature! I had been drugged, and while in a stupor made to sign my name; and my whole fortune was gone. The Colonel, who, it seems, was notorious as a most accomplished blackleg, was advertised for, but was never caught.

"I had now to give up my rooms in the hotel, and all my refined habits, take lodgings in a street near Drury Lane, and seek for some way of earning my bread. Surely, I thought, I can't starve: in this immense community there must be many thousands of vacant situations. But I did not take into account, that for every single vacancy there must be at least ten applicants. And I very soon found that the education which I had got at school and at the university, and which had cost so much, was practically useless. In fact, it was now the great stumbling-block in my way. It had not fitted me for the higher situations, for I could not even spell correctly; and it had *un*fitted me for the lower situations, for no one would engage an Oxford scholar for a menial office. I could not even compete with the ragged street boys in running on an errand, holding a horse, or sweeping a crossing. Their education, picked up amid the mud and jostle of the streets, had been far more practical and effective than mine. Instead, therefore, of living by my labour, I was obliged to subsist by pawning my valuables, and bit after bit of my finery, like the plumes of a moulting peacock, dropped from me, till I was left almost bare. Then I was obliged to give up my lodgings, and go out on the streets.

"I was now an outcast in London. It seemed strange that in the midst of so many thousand houses, I should be without a corner to lay my head in,—that in the midst of millions of people I should not have a single one to help me, or take an interest in me. Such was my condition on a night of August last. I had a few shillings in my pocket, but as I did not see any way by which I could earn money, it was necessary to be rigidly economical. I applied for a night's shelter at a cheap lodging-house in the Borough, but it was so crowded with shabby, dirty, and noisy lodgers that I turned sick, and was obliged to leave. I then tried the casual ward in one of the infirmaries, but it was even more disgusting. Quite at a loss to know what to do, I wandered aimlessly up and down till I found myself on London Bridge, when the steeples were pealing out the hour of midnight. Footsore and weary, I threw myself down on the hard stone seat in one of the recesses; but shortly, a poor, slouching tatterdemalion squatted down beside me, actually laying his unkempt head upon my legs. In disgust, I started up, and crawled away into the city. Hour after hour I dragged my weary limbs along the solitary, interminable streets, looking for some covered doorway where I might lay me down and sleep. Twice I had found a suitable spot; but before I could take possession of it, a policeman's lantern was seen approaching, and I was obliged to move on. When morning began to break I found myself close to Regent's Park, and the soft green sward appeared a temptation which I could not resist. Climbing the fence with some difficulty, I made for a large beech tree, and pillowing my head on one of its extended roots, and stretching out my legs on the soft delightful grass, I fell at once into a deep slumber.

"After several hours of absolute unconsciousness, I had a dream, and thought I was back again in Scotland, in our garden at Eskbank, and heard somebody calling to me. I gradually came to myself, and opened my eyes; and there was a working-man standing over me, and, in an accent unmistakably Scotch, calling me by name, and asking why I was there. I cannot describe the gush of delight that ran through me when I heard the kindly tones of my native land, and realised that here at least was a man who took an interest in me. Raising myself up, I asked him how he came to know me? He told me that he belonged to Eskbank, that he used to know me by sight, that he was on his way to his work in Regent Park Gardens, and that he was astonished to see me lying like an outcast there. What could I do but tell him my sad story? He said that it might be a long time before I could get any suitable berth in London, and that my best plan would be to go home at once, and that he would lend me five shillings—all that he had on him—to help me on my way. My heart bounded with delight at the suggestion, and I wondered that I had never thought of it before. So, taking his offered loan, and along with it his address, and promising to repay him as soon as I was able, I shook hands with my humble friend, and set off at once to prepare for my journey. Not having enough money to pay the fare either by coach or boat, I resolved to go on foot, and hoped that by taking every precaution, I would not find it too much for me, and that I might be able to get some odd jobs by the road, which would assist my expenses. So I packed up all my effects in a napkin, and bravely set my face to the north.

"When, from the top of Highgate, I had taken my last look of the smoky wilderness called London, and when I turned to go forward through the rich autumn landscape, I felt really happy.

After my bitter experience of the endless rows of brick houses, and the everlasting stone pavement, I enjoyed the long lines of leafy trees and hedges, and the soft, fragrant wayside grass. The very thought that every step was taking me nearer home was a delight in itself. That the distance was four hundred miles did not seem to matter much. Our school's sports, especially that of hounds and hare, had taught me to hold in, and not expend all my resources at once. So I moved along at a steady, regular pace, taking care not to strain my muscles. When my feet grew hot, I refreshed them by walking into a brook. When faintness came on, I did not seek the ale-house; but I bought a penny loaf, and sitting down by a wayside well, found that plain bread and water were both palatable and invigorating. For dessert, I sometimes had a young Swedish turnip, which I found more sweet and juicy than any pine-apple I ever tasted. At night, as the weather continued remarkably dry and warm, I preferred the open air to the tramp's lodging-house; and under the newly-cut corn sheaves, or in the recess of a haystack, I slept soundly till I was wakened by the rising sun.

"With all my economy, however, my little

stock of money melted fast away; and I soon saw that if I wished to be saved from the degradation of begging I must earn something. I therefore hit upon a plan which I thought would be sure to get me some employment. This was to call upon the clergymen through whose parishes I passed, to tell them frankly the cause of my degradation, and to ask them in the name of Christian charity to allow me to do some work for them, by which I could earn a meal or a small sum of money. But, unfortunately, this patent plan of mine failed. Without exception, the parish priests listened to my story with an incredulous look, shook their heads, and shut their doors in my face. At length I ventured to ask one why he disbelieved me?

"'My good man,' he said, 'I can't help it. I have been so often taken in by people like you. The more plausible your story is, the more likely it is to be false.'

"'You look upon poverty, then,' said I, 'as a crime?'

"'No,' he replied, 'not exactly, but as one of the marks of a criminal. I may be wrong, but I can't help it.'

"I saw, too, that my fellow-tramps had the

same opinion about me. One evening, at a sudden turn of the road, I found myself face to face with one of a most villainous type. There was no mistaking him. He was a real London-made rough, spawned in the gutter, bred in the slums, moulded in the jostle of the streets, with plunder in his look and blasphemy on his tongue.

"Planting himself right before me, and devouring me with his rat-like eyes, he croaked out, 'Well, my bloomin' cove! what lay are you on?'

"I told him that I was a gentleman who had been unfortunate in London, and was now on my way back to my native country.

"'Oh! a gent are you?' he said, with a sneer; 'then, by ——, fork out like a gent;' and he seized me by the coat collar.

"And now, for the first time, I found I had been taught at school something that was useful. Throwing off his hand, I leapt back, and put myself in a boxing attitude; and, as he made a furious assault upon me, I parried his blows, and letting go my left straight from the shoulder, landed on his jaw a crashing blow which sent him to the grass; and there he lay half-stunned, and looking like a heap of filthy clothes. I asked him if he would have any more, and getting nothing but a terrible imprecation in reply, I left him, and went on my way.

"By this time I had passed Newark, and I was in a sorry plight. I was without shoes and without a waistcoat, and my hat was crushed and battered out of all shape. With bleeding feet and empty stomach, I was limping along painfully, when I came to a farmer superintending his reapers near the roadside. Touching my forehead, I asked him if he could not give a starving man a job by which he could earn a bite of bread.

"'No lad,' he said, 'but if ye had coomed when the taters were young I could have given you a job. I might have employed you as a scarecrow.'

"Thereupon all the workers laughed, especially the women, who sent up a loud skirl of delight. So I had to crawl on, footsore, and also heartsore at the cruelty of my fellow-creatures.

"But relief was at hand. I had not gone far, when, turning a corner of the road, I came upon a strange sight: a fat little man, with a red coat, and a red face, both discoloured by the weather, sitting at the edge of a wood, eating his dinner, with his little dog in front of him, and his properties — a Punch and Judy show, a big drum, and Pandean pipes — indistinctly seen in the foliage behind him. He was eating bread and cheese, which he cut with a clasp-knife, and Toby was eyeing him greedily, ready to snap his occasional bit. Everything about the man was so hearty, and so suggestive of sunshine and country roads, that he seemed to warm up the landscape.

"As soon as he caught sight of me he called out, 'Hallo, mate! you seem done up. Come and peck a bit. Sit down.' And he handed me a big hunk of bread and another of cheese, looking on beamingly when I devoured it; and when at length I could eat no more, he produced a flask.

"'Here is some of the right sort; take a good swig of it; it will oil your digestion works. Man! it does me good to see you enjoy your grub. I feel as if I were eating a second dinner. Now for your yarn.' Then he lit his pipe and smoked while I gave an account of myself.

"'Ah,' he said, knocking out the ashes, 'my case is not altogether unlike yours. I, too, got a good education, or what was intended to be a good education. But I could never settle in any place. By nature I was a rolling stone, or rather a rolling ball of fat; and Fortune, mistaking me for a football, began to kick me about, and has been playing with me ever since. But thanks to my fat, I always fall soft and always rebound. Ha! ha!' and he laughed till his face puckered up and showed his eyes like two small steel beads.

"While he was talking, I had taken up the Pandean pipes, and I now played a tune on them.

"'Ah!' he said, 'can you work that?'

"'Yes,' I replied; 'when I was a boy in Edinburgh, there was nothing I so much delighted in as a Punch and Judy performance. I used to loiter for hours at the foot of the Mound, and see it repeated again and again; and coming upon a set of Pandean pipes in my father's pawnshop, I used to practise upon them.'

"'Why,' said Joe Greener (for, as I learnt afterwards, this was his name), 'you're the very man I want. Aint it lucky? To tell you the truth, I'm in a bit of a fix. My pal bolted two days ago with all the swag. A good riddance at the price.' (And here Joe abandoned himself to his peculiar snigger. He seemed to laugh all his trouble away, and blow it off as if with a gust of merriment.)

"'I have written,' he continued, 'for an old partner in London, but he can't come for some weeks. Meanwhile you'll do for a substitute. I'll soon coach you up in the business. All that you have got to do is to play the overture before the drama begins, and while it is going on to collect the money and keep the imps of children from pulling aside the baize and peeping in. The terms are six bob a week and your grub; and I'll advance something at once to rig you out.'

"The bargain was struck; and that evening, in the inn yard of the neighbouring village, we had several rehearsals, and I felt that I would manage to get through my part fairly well.

"Behold me now, an Oxford man, and formerly the chum of lords and swells, degraded into a Punch and Judy assistant. It was a bustling life. We were out in the road in all weathers, performing at fairs, and in the evenings in small towns and villages. In fact, wherever we saw groups of people hanging about on the outlook for amusement, we set up our stage. Once we were hired to amuse the boys at my old school, Vere de Vere College. I cannot describe the feelings with which, in my new character, I entered the well-known scenes. My uppermost feeling was the fear lest I should be identified as a former scholar. But, to my infinite relief, I saw that all the pupils and the servants were strangers. The doctor, indeed, stared at me for a moment as if he recognised me; but he turned away, muttering 'No, no, impossible!' He could not believe that anyone who had had the unspeakable advantage of being taught by him could possibly have fallen so low. His conceit saved me.

"This vagrant life had its drudgery and its difficulties; but there were certain things about it that I liked very much: the quiet country roads, the resting on the green grass under hawthorn hedges, the palatable dinners of bread and cheese and cider at rustic inns, and the merry faces that clustered round us when that abandoned rascal Punch began to play his pranks. But, at the end of a few weeks, Joe Greener's former pal arrived from London, and my occupation was gone. So, bidding a hearty farewell to my merry benefactor, I turned my face northwards again, and partly by walking and partly by coaching, I have come thus far.

"When I arrived at your gate to-night, and listened to the well-remembered sound of the wind in the big plane tree, the past came back upon me, and I felt as if I were a boy again, and as if my strange experiences at Oxford and London were but the medley of a dream."

"Bless me," cried Miss Grizzie, "did you ever live here?" and she and her sister were on their feet scrutinising the face of the stranger.

"Yes," he said quietly; "I once lived in this very house, and I can give you a proof of it. Look at the back of the fireplace there, on the left-hand side, and you will see the letters B. L. cut in a stone." They all crowded round the fire to look; and, surely enough, they detected the initials, badly formed and rather indistinct, but still recognisable.

Then Miss Lizzie, turning round and looking intently at the stranger, called out, "Are you Ben Levy? Eh! I thocht that there was something about yer face that I should ken. Ah! I mind ye weel—a bit laddie, comin' ower here in yer vakens, and introducin' yersel as oor coosin, and steyin' for three or four weeks."

"But yer faither," said Miss Grizzie, "was a gentleman, I thocht. I never heard o' him bein' a pawnbroker."

"No," said Ben, "he had retired by that time from the three balls, and wished them to be forgotten."

Hillend, now putting his hand on the shoulder of the stranger, said, "Oh man! is this you? Man, I'm fain to see ye. I mind ye weel—an auld-farrant loon, dour at the readin', writin', and coontin', but ready with yer haunds, and in the thick of everything—howin', shearin', and threshin', —and wi' an awfu' wark wi' bease. An' have ye really been through a' thae ups and doons: and what are ye gaun to dae noo?"

"Well," said Ben, "that's just what I want to tell you. You see I have had my chances—all the advantages which a man could have—education, society, money. I could not use them, and they nearly did for me. They have been a curse to me. I don't want them again. It is evident that my proper sphere is a humble lot in the country. I shall be content if anybody allows me to work in the fields, and gives me in return bed and board and a suit of clothes once a year. A man who has frequently supped on a turnip and slept under a hedge, will look upon a cog of oatmeal porridge and a bunch of straw in the barn as real luxuries."

Hillend's eyes glistened. "Well," he thought, "here's something new at a farmer's fireside, a man that has gaen up and doon the hale ladder o' Fortune, and kens a' the changes o' Life. What a companion he will be for the long winter nichts! A' the tales o' the Borders in one livin' edition! A well that can always be pumped, and will never gang dry! I think we must ask him to stey for a week or twa at least."

He gave a significant glance at his sisters, and they returned it. Then he said—"Ye micht stey on here for a wee till ye can look aroond ye. It happens that Jamie Doo, oor orra man, has just left. Ye can tak his place, and pit oot your haund to ony job that's wanted; and ye'se get a bed in the bothy, and your share o' the parritch and kail that's gaun in the kitchen."

Weeks, months, and even years passed, and Ben Levy still remained at the farm. The truth is that they could not do without him. He was the factotum of Hillend, and also of the two sisters. During the day, if any stress of work arose, he was the man to push it through; and in the evening, if any visitors dropt in, he was the man to entertain them with his startling experiences.

One remark he always made at the end of his story. "It's strange that a few weeks experience of country labour in my boyhood should have been more useful to me than all my school and university education. It has enabled me to earn my bread. I believe it's because my heart was in it.

"'The heart's aye the part aye
That maks us richt or wrang.'"

THE ONE FATAL MISTAKE.

IN my boyhood I was familiar with a thin emaciated man, that used to be seen in the streets of Sandyriggs. Consumption had wasted his body, and utterly quenched his spirit. Wan and dumb, he moved among the healthy faces of the town folk like a ghost; and it was a painful sight to see him crawl up the outside stair that led to his solitary room above the butcher's shop. People called him "a blighted being" and "a living wreck," and associated his name with a tragedy which had long been the talk of the county. Yet, twenty years before, he began his career under the most favourable auspices.

When Malcolm Blair entered the University of St Andrews, he might have been considered a favourite of Fortune. He was the only son and the pride of his father, a prosperous farmer. His body was healthy and handsome, and his mind agile and enthusiastic. He had a keen relish, not only for material blessings, but for knowledge of every kind. It was as pleasant to him to study as to take a bracing morning walk. Without any difficulty he drank in classics, mathematics, literature, and science. In all the college competitions he easily took the first place, and at the end of every session came out the first man of his year.

At the same time, his learning did not make him moody and unsocial. He put it (to use a homely phrase) "into a good skin." It was thoroughly digested, became part of his being, promoted his general health, and fed his buoyant spirits. When the time came for tossing aside his books, mirth danced in his eyes and rioted in his laugh. His motto seemed to be "Taste life's glad moments." At all the students' recreations—the social gatherings on the Friday night, the Saturday excursions into the country, the jolly junketings at Guardbridge and at Leuchars—he was the life of the company. He could sing, recite, tell stories, make a speech or "screamer," as it was called, and give the most ludicrous imitation of the different professors.

"Blair," said one of his friends, "is irrepressible.

How does he keep up that vivid tone, both of body and mind? One would imagine that his food was ambrosia and his drink was nectar; and the air which he breathed was laughing-gas."

Altogether Blair was a youth full of promise, and apparently destined for a popular and successful career.

But it was this highly-strung excitable temperament that brought him into danger. The time came, towards the end of his Arts curriculum at St Andrews, when "the young man's fancy lightly turned to thoughts of love." If he had been privileged to mix in cultured family life, his fancy might have settled on a suitable object. But in St Andrews, where the distinctions of caste are strongly defined, the students are unfortunately placed. They are regarded as being beneath the upper or professional class; and they consider themselves as above the under or trading class. They are, therefore, shut out from family life, and are left to herd together in their lodgings. And thus it came to pass that Malcolm Blair's fancy was unable to find a resting-place till it settled on his landlady's daughter.

Grace Bourhill, daughter of Mrs Bourhill,

lodging-house keeper in College Street, had no special charms beyond a fresh complexion and a pair of bright eyes. But she was ambitious, and tried all her little fascinations on Mr Blair. When she brought in his meals, she was always tidy as Hebe herself or neat-handed Phyllis. When he spoke to her, she would blush and smile and look at him from the corner of her eyes. When she ran against him in the lobby, she would show the prettiest confusion, and after begging pardon, would trip away like a startled fawn. As a matter of course, he soon saw that the girl was fond of him, and could not help appreciating her good feeling and taste. He found a pleasure in looking upon her and speaking to her, and when he was singing Burns's songs, he would often call up her image to help him to realise the poet's heroines. Yet all the while he never once thought of her as a suitable partner for him. He considered the whole affair as an innocent flirtation. Miserable delusion! He soon found out his mistake.

Blair's curriculum was drawing to a close. He was about to take farewell of St Andrews' University. As he was preparing himself for the Dissenting Ministry, his divinity studies were to be prosecuted in Edinburgh. It was a time of great excitement among the students. The winter, with its dull days and its hard work, had gone; and the spring, with its bright hours and its prospect of country holidays, had come. Song and laughter were in the air, and infected every one; and the evenings were entirely given up to farewell merry-meetings. One of the most important of these was the *Gaudeamus* of the Literary Society, held in the Cross Keys Hotel. The chair was taken by an honorary member, a divinity student of jovial tendencies; and a galaxy of youthful faces, all glowing with intelligence and good humour, was grouped before him. What could be the result but an utter abandonment to the influence of the time? The past, with all its trials, was forgotten; the future, with its promised happiness, was taken for granted; and the present, with its grateful pleasures, engrossed their whole souls.

Prominent among the company was Malcolm Blair. He was, in a certain sense, the hero of the evening. He had just completed his literary course with the greatest distinction, having taken his degree of Master of Arts with special commendation, and come out the first man of his year in every branch; and he had, therefore, every reason for being in the highest spirits. During dinner his jokes and anecdotes kept up a constant roar. After dinner he sang songs and proposed toasts in the most effective style. And then to crown all, he was called upon by the voice of the whole company to give his imitation of Tammy, the mathematical professor. Standing up, and putting on the well-known grimaces, awkward gestures, and broad Scotch accent, he delivered a speech on elocution, urging them all to cultivate a correct and refined style of speaking, and to take an example from him, the speaker, who, though born and brought up in Fife, had so thoroughly got rid of his native peculiarities of phrase and accent, that he defied any stranger to detect even his nationality. He sat down amid a prolonged shout of applause; and on every side he was saluted with cries of "Health and Imitation," and with pressing calls from dozens of his admirers to drink with them.

Replying to these on the spur of the moment, he imbibed more than he was aware of; and thus it happened, when the meeting broke up, that he was in a state of the highest excitement.

This state of excitement was, indeed, very unfortunate. But another unfortunate circumstance was fated to happen. On that particular night, of all nights in the year, it chanced that his landlady, Mrs Bourhill, was seized with a sort of fit; and when he reached his lodgings, he witnessed a most distressing plight — the mother lying insensible on the sofa, and the daughter wringing her hands and crying in despair. Alarm and pity took possession of his heart; and after uttering a few words of sympathy and comfort, he rushed away and brought back a doctor. The doctor, a young man beginning practice, was solemn and taciturn. Asking a few questions, and feeling the pulse of Mrs Bourhill, he looked very grave, and tried one restorative after another until at length she opened her eyes; and then, with the aid of the daughter, he led her to her bedroom and shut the door.

Blair retired to his own room to wait the result. The minutes passed slowly without a single sound to break the oppressive silence. At last he heard the doctor go, and shut the outer door; but he waited in vain for any other sound. Sick of suspense, and imagining all sorts of evil, he crept quietly out of his room and entered the parlour; and there he found Miss Bourhill seated on a chair, the picture of silent misery.

"What has happened?" he asked, in a voice of alarm.

She answered by breaking down into a paroxysm of weeping.

"For God's sake, Miss Bourhill," he cried, "what has happened? Is your mother dead?"

Then she rose, and with her hair streaming over her shoulders, and the tears running down her cheeks, she clasped his hands, and said, "Oh, Mr Blair! you have been so kind. But what am I to do? what *am* I to do? The doctor says that mother's condition is very serious, and that another attack may be fatal, and I shall be left alone in the world with nobody to care for me." And here she broke down again.

Now, what could this unsophisticated lad do, wrought up as he was by various causes into a high state of excitement? What could he do but take her hand, and pat her on the shoulder, and, in his anxiety to soothe her, protest that he would take care of her? And other tender promises he made which he was afterwards told about, but which he did not remember.

Next morning he awoke with a curious, confused feeling which cannot be described. Amid all the confusion, however, there still started up the impression that he had said to Miss Bourhill many things which he ought not to have said. He feared, in fact, that he had given her the impression that he really loved her; and he resolved to lose no time in disabusing her mind. He would represent it as an ordinary flirtation, and would apologise most earnestly and humbly for trifling with her feelings. He was not going to allow his future prospects to be blighted, and he must set himself right at once, and at all hazards. But, unfortunately, this resolute plan of his was utterly foiled by unforeseen circumstances. No sooner had he stepped out of his bedroom into the passage than Miss Bourhill, radiant with the consciousness of one who was both loving and beloved, and looking really beautiful, had thrown her arms around his neck and was embracing him; and her mother, glowing with recovered health, came up and saluted him also.

"Mother," said the daughter, "this is my future husband."

And the mother, blessing them fervently, protested that he was the very one whom she herself would have chosen, and congratulated him upon his having secured such a priceless jewel.

"She canna," said she, "strum on the pianny, but she can darn stockins and mak shirts. She'll no be able to jabber French, but she'll scrub and cook and keep yer manse comfortable. And she's high-spirited too, and she'll keep the members o' the congregation in their proper places. She was jist born to be a minister's wife."

Now what could the fated Malcolm do, involved as he was in such a witches' coil! He felt that if he didn't speak out and protest at once he was lost; but the smiles, caresses, and blandishments that were rained upon him, drugged and chloroformed his powers, and literally shut his mouth; and he remained speechless and helpless. Two days afterwards, Malcolm Blair left St Andrews an engaged man. The one fatal mistake had been made.

During the six months of the summer vacation that Scotch students enjoy, Malcolm Blair had been accustomed to continue his studies under the most exhilarating circumstances. What a pleasant change it was from the closeness and monotony of St Andrews' lecture-rooms to the airy canopy and ever-changing glories of nature! And oh, the delight, at daybreak, when the ploughman drove his team afield amid the thousand melodies of morn; or at noon, when a golden haze brooded over the pastures and cornfields, and the silence was broken only by the hum of the bee; or in the evening, when the scent of flowers was in the air and the coo of the cushat came from the firry woodland—oh, the delight! to dwell upon the country scenes of the Mantuan Bard, or roll out the wingèd words of Homer, or trill " the native wood-notes wild " of the Swan of Avon. Standing on the same green earth, under the same glorious sky, and amid the same perennial influences, he was able to look at things from their point of view and in their spirit, and thus virtually to realise — to make real to himself — their thoughts and feelings regarding Nature.

But now, what a difference! He moped about the fields and hedges a blighted being. The consciousness of his calamity, like a frosty cloud, enveloped his imagination; and, seen through this cloud, the world had lost its glory. And before he had been a week at home there came from his betrothed a letter which brought the blush to his cheek. With unsteady pen and bad spelling, the poor girl had laboured to express her affection, but, alas! had only betrayed her meagre and undeveloped mind. As he read this epistle at breakfast, his mother was watching him; and he knew that she was wondering who his illiterate correspondent could be; and to give her no more ground for suspicion, he was mean enough to bribe Marjory, the servant, to bring his letters in future directly to himself, and not to lay them on the breakfast table.

One day, however, when he was superintending (or "grieving," as it was called) the haymakers, an idea struck across his brain, and instantly changed his whole mood, and filled his heart with delight. Grace, he thought, was uneducated just now, but was it necessary that she should remain so? She was naturally bright and clever, and without doubt would be eager to learn. Why should she not have the opportunity? He would earn some money by going out as a tutor, and with this money he would send her to a first-class boarding-school, where she would learn the accomplishments, manners, and graces; and thus she would become a young lady of whom anyone in his position might be proud. A fond dream which might so easily be realised!

But when, in his next letter, he had propounded his plan to Grace, she, instead of accepting it gratefully, rejected it with the utmost scorn. She had some difficulty in expressing her love, but none in giving vent to her indignation. So (she wrote) he was ashamed of her because she could not jabber a few French phrases, and hammer on the piano; and he wanted her to go to one of those boarding-schools, where nothing but what was bad could be learned. She would not go to one of these dens of wickedness; but as he was ashamed of her, she would poison herself, and her murder would lie at his door. Thus ended Blair's first and last attempt to educate his betrothed.

Three years had passed without altering the state of matters. His parents had come to know of his engagement, and he saw, by their looks, how deeply disappointed and chagrined they were. He had frequently visited Grace; and although he could not help being pleased with her affectionate greeting, yet her frequent vulgar remarks, and her mother's coarse style of joking, stung him to the quick. And now there happened a change of circumstances which stirred up within him a strange mixture of vexation and delight. The letters of Miss Bourhill came to be short and far between. He suspected that there was some new attraction engrossing her; and he asked a confidential friend in St Andrews to ascertain if this was so. His suspicion was correct. She was frequently seen with a divinity student, by name Harker, good-looking after a sort, but notoriously self-indulgent and even loose in his principles. In fact, his very name at the University seemed redolent of dissipation; and his presence among innocent young girls would have been deemed absolutely blighting. He would have looked like an obscene raven among a troop of snowy doves. This man was now Mrs Bourhill's lodger, and it was evident that Miss Grace was trying her charms upon him. The reason of this double-dealing was equally clear. As a student of the Established Church, he had the prospect of a better manse, and a larger and surer stipend, than Blair would ever possess.

This revelation threw Blair into a fever of excitement; and various feelings within him struggled for the mastery: Indignation at being jilted for such a worthless rival; shame at having been inveigled into tying himself to such a mercenary flirt; determination to do his utmost to free himself; and exultation at the prospect of being able to do so. Under the influence of this whirlpool of emotion he set out to walk to St Andrews, and was carried along at a great pace, scarcely noticing the objects that he passed, and making little of the long distance. As he drew near to the ancient city, there came into his view two figures that instantly revived his flagging feelings — Harker and Miss Bourhill returning from a walk on the links. Keeping well behind them, he dogged their footsteps, and watched with a fiendish gratification how they talked, looked into each other's faces and laughed, until they reached College Street and disappeared in Mrs Bourhill's house. Then he entered without much ceremony, received the surprise and the salutation of the two women, who were in the lobby, with a cold and stern manner, said that he wished to speak with Grace alone, and following her into the parlour, locked the door to keep the mother out.

Malcolm lost no time in giving vent to his feelings. He told her the reports that had reached him; he exposed the deplorable character of Harker; he demanded that she should break off all correspondence with this man whose touch was an insult to a woman; and he wound up by saying that she must, on the spot, and once for all, choose between him and this new admirer. He spoke with great vehemence and determination, and expected to see her completely overwhelmed with shame and confusion.

But what was his astonishment to find that this uneducated girl, with nothing but her animal cunning, was more than a match for all his culture, and was prepared to defend her conduct out and out. With the air and smile of one who was dealing with a testy and unreasonable child, she proceeded to argue the matter with him. Did he really mean to blame her, because she spoke to her mother's lodger, and because she allowed him, when he met her in the street, to walk home with her? And did he really wish her to promise not to speak to Mr Harker? They could not afford to turn him away, and as long as he remained in their rooms they could not insult him. Then, waxing righteously indignant, she demanded why he employed sneaks to tell tales of her, and why he came raging and locking the door as if he were going to murder her. The fact was, that he was ashamed of her, and wanted to pick a quarrel, and to get an excuse for throwing her off. But, thank God! although she was a poor girl, she was not without friends. Her uncle, the solicitor in Edinburgh, would see that she was not wronged. And having said all this calmly, she unlocked the door and went out.

After a rest and slight repast at the Star Hotel, Malcolm returned home full of the gloomiest thoughts. This wretched girl had come out in her true character—cunning, unscrupulous, heartless. While she claimed the liberty of throwing him off, he was not to have the liberty of throwing her off. That reference to her uncle, the solicitor, showed that the terrors of the law would be employed, if necessary, to keep him to his bargain. It was a gloomy future that was opening up before him; and for several days he wandered aimlessly about, the most melancholy of men.

But Nature takes care that a healthy young soul shall not droop for long. Like a downtrodden daisy, it revives under the influence of sunshine and shower, and opens its heart to the brightness of Spring. When weeks had passed without bringing a letter from Miss Bourhill, he became sanguine, nay, even confident. Her new flirtation was evidently prospering. Harker would soon be licensed; and, as he was glib and clever enough, he would soon get a church and marry her; and then, oh! what an ominous cloud would be lifted from his life! He would then be a free man! And so a miraculous change now came over him. His youth seemed to be restored; and he began to look with a new and fresh interest on all the old familiar scenes. His mother noticed the transformation, and knew the cause; and, as she said to her husband, "Now that the boy was himself again, the farmyard and the fields seemed brighter and pleasanter."

But unfortunately this exultation was premature. One evening towards the end of March, as he sat in the parlour reading the county paper, his eyes fell upon a paragraph which struck him like an electric shock. He tried hard to fancy that the narrative might not be true after all; but the details were given in such a circumstantial and confident manner, that he was compelled in the end to believe them. They were as follows:—

"SAD DEATH OF A STUDENT.

"On the afternoon of Friday last, two divinity students, Harker and Johnstone, set out from St Andrews for a walk in the country. As they passed through Strathkinness, they stopped for refreshment at a small inn. After a time they seemed to have grown reckless, and to have set in for serious drinking; and in rapid succession they ordered tumbler after tumbler of whisky toddy; and when the landlord, becoming alarmed, refused to supply them with any more, they left and went to another public-house, where they had several glasses of brandy. When they started to go home, they were both unsteady, especially Johnstone. Some of the villagers saw them staggering down the street, and overheard Harker abusing his companion for being drunk. Next morning, Johnstone was found lying dead by the roadside near Denbrae, between Strathkinness and St Andrews; and when Harker, who had arrived at his lodgings late on the previous night, was asked what had become of his companion, he grew confused, and could only say that he could not get him to come along, and had been obliged to leave him. On Monday, the Senatus Academicus summoned Harker before them, and, after due deliberation, passed upon him the extreme sentence of expulsion. This is a severe punishment, blighting as it does his whole future career: but a still more terrible punishment must be the reflection, that he took a poor unsophisticated youth into a public-house, deliberately set to work to make him tipsy, and then in the end left him to perish by the wayside."

As Blair read this passage, he fell back again into the Slough of Despond, and all the delight of life vanished once more. He knew that the siren, whom he now loathed and had hoped to get rid of, would fall back upon him and again cling to him; and, just as he had foreboded, in a few days came the well-known hateful scrawl, appealing in a vulgar manner to his affections. What, she went on to say, had come over him? Had he fallen in love with some milkmaid and forgotten his poor little Gracie. She had been breaking her heart, waiting for a letter from him; and all the neighbours had been noticing that she had fallen away from her clothes. Was not that a dreadful scrape Harker had got into? She was not surprised at it, knowing what a bad character he was. Though she had been obliged to be civil to him, she had always hated him. Thank goodness she would now get rid of his attentions! With a whole lot of kisses, and waiting for a letter from him, she was his own Grace.

After reading this, he gnashed his teeth with vexation and disgust, tore the letter to pieces, and threw it in the fire. He did not answer it; and he vowed that from that time he would treat her with the silent contempt she deserved.

At the end of another year, Blair was licensed to preach, and became what is called a *probationer*. He had looked forward to this as the great epoch of his life, the turning-point of his career, when he was to become the accredited legate of heaven, to bear the message of salvation to his perishing fellow-creatures. Could anyone have a nobler work? But, unfortunately, this sacred office was hampered by preliminary conditions which he felt to be exceedingly humiliating. He had first to get a church; and in order to get a church, he had to please that very uncertain thing called the popular taste. In this perplexing task, the great stores of learning which he had been piling up for so many years gave him little or no assistance. He sat down doggedly and constructed his sermon after the most approved conventional method. By persistent reiteration he committed it to memory, word for word. With fluttering heart and trembling knees he went up to the pulpit on Sunday and began to give it off. During this unwinding process, he did not see the congregation before him; but he was looking at the image of his manuscript; and his mind's eye was running over line after line and page after page. It was a recitation exercise, and not a living speech coming warm from the heart of the speaker and going direct to the heart of the hearers. And all the while, he did not feel that he was pleading with his fellow-creatures to accept the Word of God. He felt that he was really begging them to notice how ably he was treating the subject, how effectively he was delivering it, and what a promising young creature he was. He was, in fact, a sort of itinerant theological hawker, hawking his spiritual wares from town to town.

And as time went on, he found himself beaten in the bid for popularity by fellow-students who were far inferior to him in ability and scholarship. Sim, who could not for the life of him construe a Latin sentence, and Macfarlane Macdonald, who was never known to have a single idea in his head on any subject whatever, found no difficulty in tickling the ear of the many-headed beast, and became ordained ministers while he continued to wander about, an uncalled probationer. It soon became evident that Malcolm Blair, the most distinguished student of his time, was in danger of becoming "a stickit minister."

But this universe is constructed on the grand principle of compensation. Providence seldom inflicts a wound without supplying a soothing plaster. That want of success, which lands us in poverty and hardship, scares away our false friends. Miss Grace Bourhill thought herself too good to be a stickit minister's wife; and while Blair's fate hung in the balance, ceased altogether to correspond with him; and at length, to his infinite relief, he heard that she was married to a cousin of her own, a prosperous brewer in St Andrews. Freedom at last! and brought about in an unexpected way! He now gloried exceedingly in his failure as a preacher. What was the want of manse and stipend compared with the escape from that incubus which had pressed the very spirit out of him! The world now lay bright before him, and he was free to go his own way by himself. As the church did not want him, he would adopt some other calling; and he was actually preparing himself to undertake either literary or scholastic work, when he received an invitation to engage in one of the most striking enterprises of the day.

Those that knew Fife more than fifty years ago must remember Miss Singleton, who worked such wonders in the way of evangelising the mining village of Coaltown. She belonged to that strongly-marked and combative class of female social reformers; and certainly she was one of the best specimens of the class. She was not, like some of her sisterhood, conceited, arrogant, and masculine. Though she was strong-minded, she was also strong-hearted. If she was bold and aggressive, it was in urging the claims of the oppressed, and not in exhibiting her own cleverness. Her plan for raising the sunken masses was direct and drastic. "Get rid," she said to the missionary, "of all that priestly parade and formality which have concealed so long the true living face of religion. Return to Christ's sublimely simple plan, which is founded on the two everlasting facts of the Fatherhood of God and the Brotherhood of man. Imitate Him as far as the circumstances of the time will allow. Go down among the lapsed masses, not with man-millinery, patronising airs, and doles of blankets and soup, but with wisdom in your head and real love in your heart. Live amongst them, become one of themselves, and help them in their difficulties and sorrows." Such was the method which Miss Singleton herself had carried out; and the results were said to be marvellous.

This was the lady who now wrote to Malcolm Blair. "She had listened to his preaching," she said, "and had heard of him from some other friends, and she thought that he might be able to assist her in her labours. She could not give him very much in the form of money, but he might be able to find some of his reward in the work itself. Should he think favourably of this proposal, would he kindly call upon her?"

After considering this matter long and carefully, Blair came to the conclusion that he could not do better than wait upon Miss Singleton. And when he had once seen her and talked with her, he could not refuse her offer. Miss Singleton's whole personality was like a pleasing revelation to him. Instead of the bold-featured, masculine-looking woman that he expected to see, he beheld a gentle and beautiful young lady, the secret of whose power lay in her feminine tact and sympathy. And when he saw her moving about among the poor, she seemed to him the very embodiment of the spirit of Christianity. Wherever there was sickness or sorrow—that was her chosen abode. There was comfort in the sound of her voice; there was healing in her very touch. Her smile was the highest reward, and her look of painful disapproval was the heaviest punishment. In her presence the coarsest miner felt ashamed of his conduct, and silently vowed to give up swearing and drinking.

Like the rest of those who came under Miss Singleton's influence, Blair soon caught her enthusiasm. He threw himself heart and soul into the work of evangelising Coaltown, visiting the houses of the poor miners, talking with them in a brotherly way, listening to their troubles and ailments, and helping them to help themselves. There were many experiences which filled his senses with disgust, and even sickened his very soul. But there were also many surprising results which amply atoned for all his pain. What sight could be more pleasing than to see a ragged and red-faced drunkard gradually being transformed into a well-clad and intelligent man; and what sound could be more delightful than to hear the thanks of a wife and children for a husband and father reclaimed, and a home made happy?

But the most gratifying circumstance was a change in his own nature, which may seem almost miraculous, but which has happened to others, and which can easily be explained. This new evangelising work actually remedied the defects of his theological training; and "the

Back Raw" of Coaltown became a school of eloquence, and did for him what the University and Divinity Hall had been unable to do. The intimate knowledge which he there acquired of human nature filled his heart with a fuller sympathy; and this fuller sympathy let loose his power of utterance. Out of the abundance of his heart his mouth spoke. He was so eager to supply comfort and guidance that he gave no thought to his language, and his language came readily of its own accord. In preparing his Sunday discourses, there was no longer any need of slavishly writing them down and committing every word. All he had to do was to think out the subject, to arrange the details, and to trust to the inspiration of the moment for the language. The consequence was, that he drew large audiences, that his fame as a preacher soon spread abroad, and that, when he least expected such a thing, he received a call from a large dissenting congregation in the town of Easterton.

Though this call gratified him exceedingly for several reasons, and chiefly because it vindicated his character as a preacher, and took him out of the black list of stickit ministers, yet he hesitated before he accepted it. He found himself bound to Coaltown by a feeling almost stronger than life itself. In spite of its dismalness and poverty, it had become to him an enchanted ground. There was a presence which brightened the landscape; there was a voice which diffused a holy calm through the air; and this presence and this voice belonged to Miss Singleton. She was the daybreak that had arisen upon his night of despondency, and had filled the world with light and melody; and to part from her was to go back into darkness again. And when he spoke about his dilemma to herself, he found that she was just as much affected as he was. With tears in her eyes, she confessed that she would miss him very much.

However, just when he was on the point of asking why they should part, and why they should not continue to work together as husband and wife, she rallied both herself and him to a sense of duty. This call, she said, had brought a great opportunity of applying the system to the degraded classes of a large town, which might never occur again. It was an epoch in his life: it might be an epoch in the history of Christianity. He must, therefore, throw all other considerations aside, and accept it. Meanwhile at least, they must deny themselves all other pleasures. Self-denial was necessary to their spiritual life. It was the manna which kept them alive in this wilderness of a world.

Malcolm Blair, accordingly, had no other alternative than to accept the call; and at the end of a few weeks had to tear himself away from Coaltown. His only consolation (and it was a great one, filling his soul with the highest hopes) was that Miss Singleton had shown that she was most tenderly attached to him.

The 27th of April was set apart for his ordination by the Presbytery in the dissenting church of Easterton. It was a day that was doomed to be memorable to him for ever. At the beginning of the ceremony he was in a melancholy mood. He had been overworking himself, had fainted more than once, and felt weak and nervous. As he sat under the pulpit, looking out upon the crowded pews, he saw nothing in the faces of his new congregation save staring curiosity; and away to the right was a dark countenance full of settled hate. He knew who it was. It was the Rev. Ewan Murdoch, who had been his fellow-student at St Andrews, and had been known as "Dark Murdoch," and who had been one of the unsuccessful candidates for the pulpit of the present congregation.

"If I have a mortal enemy," said the new minister to himself, "there he sits, one of those wretched beings who look upon the success of a fellow-creature as an unpardonable injury."

Towards the conclusion of the service, however, Malcolm passed into a better mood. The preacher's sermon on the text, "Fellow-workers with God," spoke words of encouragement that went to his heart. The first line of the concluding psalm was, "Unto the upright light doth rise," and no sooner was it read than an outburst of sunshine flooded the building. Then, when the congregation in a long line passed before him to give him the right hand of fellowship, there was warmth in every smile and in every grip. And amongst them, what should he see but the face of Miss Singleton! He was so delighted that he compared her to an angel bringing with her the atmosphere of heaven.

"Miss Smeaton and I," said she, "came this morning. We must make some calls in the town, and then we shall drop in at the manse to have a cup of tea and a long chat."

He left the church full of hope and happiness.

As he walked up the High Street, it was with a springy step, so that the gossips standing on the stairheads remarked what a pleasant-looking, active man he was. And when he entered the manse garden at Highfield, he thought that he had never seen a more charming place. The house stood on a site commanding an extensive view of the Firth of Forth, with the castle and spires of Edinburgh distinct against the horizon; and the garden in front, with its green gooseberry bushes and apple trees, sloped towards the sunny south. There, too, in the doorway of his new abode, stood his mother, now in widow's weeds, who had brought herself and her furniture to make a home for him. Truly he thought, "the lines had fallen to him in pleasant places." And after a comfortable lunch, they had a long confidential talk, in which he told about Miss Singleton's intended visit, and gave a glowing account of Miss Singleton herself, and hinted that he intended to ask her to be his wife.

"Then, oh! happiness," he said, "for us three to live in this paradise together! What a blessed helper she will be in my work, and what a kind housekeeper and guardian you will make! It is a prospect almost too good for this world."

They were still talking when the servant came in to say that two ladies were in the drawing-room wishing to see the minister. Malcolm started up, radiant with joy.

"Bring them in here," he cried. "Now, mother, you will see my dearest friend, and, I hope, my future wife."

But, horror of horrors! who should be announced and ushered in but Mrs and Miss Bourhill, the mother and daughter who had been such familiar figures in his nightmare of the past. As the terrible significance of this reappearance dawned upon him, it seemed to strike him to the heart, and he fell back in a swoon.

When he recovered consciousness, he found himself propped up in an easy chair, and saw four women standing round him in a state of silent excitement. Miss Singleton, pale and pensive, was gazing intently at him; the two Bourhills were staring at Miss Singleton with an expression of indignant surprise; and his mother, full of keenest anxiety, divided her attention between him and the others.

Miss Singleton broke the silence by saying—"I must go. We strangers had better leave the invalid to quiet and the care of his mother."

"Thank you, my dear lady," said his mother, "for that sensible remark."

"But," said Miss Bourhill, "that remark does not apply to me, his betrothed."

"Nor to me," added Mrs Bourhill, "his mother-in-law to be."

"Dear me," said Mrs Blair to Miss Bourhill, "you are married, you know. We saw it in the papers."

"A mistake," replied Miss Bourhill, "a cousin of the same name, not me."

"But," pleaded Mrs Blair, "the engagement fell to the ground. The correspondence stopped years ago."

"Malcolm's fault," replied Miss Bourhill quietly. "I wrote last."

"A promise," added Mrs Bourhill, "can't be broken but by the consent of both parties. A bargain's a bargain."

These replies, curt and remorseless, sounded in the young minister's ears like his death-knell, and he lay back in his chair and closed his eyes in mute agony.

But Malcolm Blair, enfeebled though he was, was too brave to be crushed at once. In a few days his mind had regained its strength, and was calmly looking the difficulty in the face. He had, he saw, just two alternatives. One was to hold himself bound by his blindfold engagement, to marry Miss Bourhill, and so to blight his whole future career: the other was to break his promise and bravely take the consequences— a law suit, a public exposure of all his private affairs, the payment of heavy damages, and the resignation of the position to which he had just been appointed. The latter course was the one which he was inclined to take. But before definitely deciding, he wrote to Miss Singleton stating his resolution, and giving his reasons for it. The engagement between him and Miss Bourhill, he argued, was made in a moment of excitement, and when they were both young and thoughtless. Any affection they might have had for each other was a mere fancy, and very soon vanished. By a tacit agreement they ceased to write to each other, and for years there had been no correspondence between them. To go through the solemn and binding rite of marriage under these circumstances would be to lay the crime of perjury upon their souls. This argument seemed to Malcolm to be so unanswerable, that he felt sure of the approval of Miss Singleton.

Great, therefore, was his surprise when he received a letter from her expressing her deep regret that she could not approve of his resolution. The exchange of the heart's affection, she said, between a man and a woman was a serious and solemn engagement. It was often a matter of life and death. Not only the happiness of the individuals themselves, but the welfare of society might depend upon it. It was really as binding as the marriage vow itself. No cooling of affection, no temporary estrangement, nothing but infidelity could be a reason for setting it aside. And as for his future happiness, he should not despair. By the use of tender and assiduous sympathy he had succeeded in rekindling healthy affection in many a degraded soul. Why should the influence which had been so effectual in the slums of Coaltown fail at his own fireside. Let him keep his promise like an honourable man and a Christian. Let him do the right, and trust in God for the result.

When Malcolm Blair was reading this letter, he felt like a criminal receiving sentence of death. Had anyone else than Miss Singleton offered this opinion, he would have spurned it. But she was his guardian angel, one who, in his belief, had never erred, and could never err. Besides, if he did what she considered a dishonourable action, he would forfeit her approval; and that was all the world to him. He therefore felt himself bound to follow her advice, although he broke his heart in doing it. He even forced himself to take up her sanguine view of the future, and hoped that by kind and sympathetic treatment, he would succeed in making Grace Bourhill into a useful minister's wife.

Four years have elapsed — four momentous years. Mr and Mrs Blair are seated at breakfast. He is wan and wasted, and stoops over his cup and plate as he drinks his weak tea and eats his thin toast. She is stout, red, and restless-eyed. A pervading air of discomfort is given to the room by the dirty discoloured tablecloth, the disarranged furniture, and the careless dress of the two occupants. The following is the conversation which passes between them.

"There!" says she, tossing to her husband a letter which she has just opened and glanced over, "there's Goodsir's, the grocer's account."

"Good heavens!" replied he, staring at it and turning pale.

"Don't swear."

"Sixty-four pounds seventeen and eightpence! and of that, thirty pounds odd for wine! We must really do with less wine."

"You say *we*, meaning that I have consumed most of it. You grudge me the glass of port which the doctor ordered."

"My dear! have I not often pressed you to take it?"

"You forget the wine you give away to your paupers."

"I can't see my poor sick fellow-creatures perishing without sharing with them the best that I have."

"You smuggled two bottles away last night in your greatcoat pocket."

"Yes, and if I can save poor widow Slight to her young family, and Robbie Stark to his distracted parents, my reward will be great."

"You forget, too, the bottles which you sent to your mother. She is the greatest pauper of them all. She wanted to live here to sorn upon us; but I soon sent her to the right about."

"My dear, is it kind, is it Christian-like to use such language?"

"You never send any to *my* mother."

"Your mother is strong. Besides, you forget the yearly allowance that I pay to her."

"If I do forget it, it's not for want of it being cast up to me. Why don't you ask for a rise of stipend?"

"My dear, I could not, through sheer shame, do such a thing. My poor people are severely taxed already to make up my salary. There's Sandy Slack, with ten shillings a week and six children, giving one shilling a month toward my maintenance. Upon my word, I'm ashamed to look the poor man in the face."

"Why don't you look out for a better situation?"

"No, no, no! I could not go about like a hireling, offering myself to the highest bidder. I would forfeit my own self-respect as well as the respect of every one in my congregation."

"Much respect they have for you when they insult your wife as they do."

"No, no, not insult."

"You know they do. I'm sure (*shedding tears*) when I came here I tried to do my duty as a minister's wife. I went among the poor and gave them the benefit of my advice. And what was my reward? That man, Kinnell, because I found fault with him for giving his children tea instead of porridge, turned me to the door, and I became the laughing-stock of the whole congregation."

"Unfortunately, your zeal carried you away. In dealing with these people we must come down to their level, and look at things from their point of view."

"Come down to their level, indeed! I should be sorry to do so. And then the big folk of your congregation! You can't say that I did not come down to their level. And what did I bring upon myself? One day at afternoon tea at Lady Brockie's, I heard her friends, Mrs Soutar and Mrs Stables, call her Sarah, and I followed suit. You should have seen her face. She was never the same afterwards; and now she never invites me along with you. I'm not good enough for your grand friends."

"My dear, we all receive slights. You should be like those who have given themselves up to mission work. They look upon such slights as part of the cross they have to bear."

"I know what you mean. You were about to say I should be like your precious Miss Singleton. You are constantly casting her up."

"My dear! I never mentioned her name."

"That makes it all the more suspicious. You are constantly thinking of her. Don't deny it. I tell you I *know* it; and I know your ongoings with her at Coaltown. Mr Murdoch told me. And I know that on the day of your ordination you were waiting for her, in the manse here, to propose to her, when I dropped in, in time to spoil the sport. Ha! ha! you wonder how I found that out. Your mother let the cat out of the bag. And you got a letter from her this morning. I detected the handwriting. If there's nothing wrong, why do you hide it?"

"I did not hide it. I was just going to show it to you. There it is. Read it."

"What? coming here to-day at eleven (*starting to her feet*); she sha'n't come here. Not so long as *I*'m here. I'll tell the servant not to let her in."

"I will certainly countermand that order."

"Then I'll go to the door myself and slam it in her face."

"And I will certainly take means to prevent you. Listen to me. I'm speaking quite calmly. That venomous man, Murdoch, who told you about the ongoings of Miss Singleton and myself, is a slanderer. Our whole souls were in our mission work. Every word exchanged between us was about it, and might have been published to the world. She comes here to-day as a servant of God, interested in God's work, and I would be a heartless, graceless coward if I allowed my door to be shut in her face. Now let that be understood. Let that be understood."

Mr Blair sits waiting for a reply. His wife, however, preserves an unusual silence, and sits staring into vacancy with a fixed look. He does not like this, as it is so uncommon with her, and he anticipates a stormy scene. But to his infinite surprise, when the door bell sounds, she does not get up; and when Miss Singleton is ushered in, she rises and shakes hands with her, and goes out of the room saying that she will bring her a cup of tea. And then comes a scene which can never cease to haunt his memory! He feels himself to be in a sort of trance, seeing horrible deeds swiftly done before him, desiring to prevent them, but utterly unable to do so. He and his visitor have scarcely exchanged the usual inquiries regarding health, before he sees his wife enter with a cup. He sees her give it to Miss Singleton;

he sees Miss Singleton receive it with a smile; before he can cry out to her, "Don't drink it," he sees her take several sips; he sees her fall back lifeless; he sees his wife throw her arms into the air with a demoniac gesture of delight; and he sees and hears no more.

When he comes to his senses, he is conscious of the presence of several people, and hears Sir Benjamin Brockie's voice, very much broken down and full of tears. This hard, unsympathetic man, generally so replete with narrow opinions, and so stubborn in maintaining them, is, by some strong influence, quite softened. The flinty rock has been touched as if by the prophet's rod, and the pure waters of Christian charity flow forth.

"This excellent woman," he is saying, "has died a martyr. She had heard of Mr Blair's unhappy married life, and she came over expressly to try and put things right. She called upon me to see how the land lay, and she thought that we had been lacking in sympathy towards Mrs Blair. All that we want, she said, to regenerate mankind is enough of sympathy. Sympathy is the great sanitary agent in the moral world. If applied in large enough measure, it will neutralise every evil, and sweeten the social atmosphere. She had great hopes that she would make all right; and I believe that she would have succeeded had she not been so suddenly cut off by the unfortunate woman whom she was trying to save. I don't know how it was, but her own example seemed to be a mirror in which other people saw how defective they were. For my own part, I felt to-day, after seeing her, that I and my family, and the rest of the congregation, had been remiss in our duty towards Mr and Mrs Blair; and I hurried over to lose no time in atoning for my mistake."

The sight of the best and purest being whom he had ever known, murdered before his eyes by the woman who bore his name, was never to be forgotten by Malcolm Blair. It haunted his soul like a spectre, would give him no rest, and wasted his strength away. For many weeks he lay prostrate, hovering between life and death; and during his hours of delirium, when his judgment no longer kept the door of his heart, his feelings wandered forth at will, and those waiting at his bedside heard him express repugnance for his wife, and call in agonising tones for a glimpse of Julia Singleton's face. He recovered enough of strength to be able to rise from his bed, but it was only to find himself alone and helpless. His wife was a hopeless lunatic in a private asylum; his aged mother, crushed by the misfortunes of her dear son, was dead; and he felt himself called upon to resign his pleasant manse, and to retire to the solitary lodging at Sandyriggs in which I knew him.

At first, he felt that his Divine Master had no more work for him, and that all that remained for him was to lie down and die. But by and by Milton's noble lines occurred to him:

" Who best
Bear His mild yoke, they serve Him best : His state
Is kingly : thousands at His bidding speed,
And post o'er land and ocean without rest;
They also serve who only stand and wait."

And thus he waited patiently till Death, the remover of all burdens and the solver of all difficulties, came to his release.

A ROMANCE OF THE HARVEST FIELD.

A LARGE field of ripe wheat surrounded by a fringe of trees; a long line of sun-brown reapers, of all ages and of both sexes, stretching across the whole breadth of the field, and bending to their work; the golden shocks falling before the gleaming sickles; and over all a warm autumnal haze.

It is a great occasion, a sort of annual festival to which people have flocked from every quarter of the country. There are solid-looking Highlanders in garments rough-spun, and smelling of peat reek; canny Aberdonians asking "far is't" and "far was't"; Edinburgh wives, with tongues so slick and sharp that (to use a vulgar phrase) they could almost "clip a clout"; well-favoured matrons and maidens from the cottages round about; and chubby boys and girls who glean, or (as they call it) "gather" among the stooks, making up their gatherings into "singles." Even the infant is there, attended by his elder sister, and kicking his heels as he lies on a couch of sheaves. There is a feeling of hilarity in the air. The thought of the higher wages they are earning, the prospect of scones and ale for lunch and dinner, the sight of the abundant harvest they are reaping, the scent of the aromatic herbs they are treading upon, and the glorious weather, all combine to gladden their hearts and let loose their tongues. They talk, they laugh, and they sing. And sometimes, in the superfluity of their spirits and strength, they take to what is called "kemping," that is to say, each *rig* or company or division of shearers tries to get before the others. In other words, there is a competition as to which band will do the most work. Strange! will workers of the present day believe this?

High above all the clamour is heard the voice of Peg Jackson, a broad-beamed, brawny virago, who is known by the expressive name of "The Bummer." She is one of that class who bring themselves into notice by virtue of a loud and glib tongue, and a bold and brazen countenance. In her remarks she is no respecter of persons. Her satire glances at all sorts of game, from

Dave, the herd boy, up to Mr Stocks, the master. Many of her phrases also are very graphic; and, like burrs, are prickly and apt to stick to the persons against whom they are cast. This self-elected oracle is engaged in disposing of some local scandal that has been brought up for her judgment, when she catches sight of the farmer, along with a gentleman and several ladies, entering the field.

"Oh," exclaims Peg, "there's Stocks himsel comin' to keep us at oor wark; and he has brocht some friens wi' him to glower at us, jist as if we were wild beasts in a show. My certie! a bonnie sicht we'll mak, raxin' and sweatin' like pownies in a mill."

"But wha's thae wi' him," asked Kate Corby, a girl from the Nethergate at Sandyriggs, who, after a few days' acquaintance, had become Peg's admirer and toady.

"Tuts, lassie, whaur hae ye been cleckit that ye dinna ken that," replied Peg. "That thing in a white frock, and wi' a face made o' skim-milk cheese, is Stocks's sister, Miss Tammy (Thomasina they ca' her when they want to speak proper). And that lanky shaver, for a' the warld like a pair o' tangs oot for a daunder, is her sweetheart, young Tosh o' Lammert's Mill. That little black-e'ed cratur in a red jacket is Miss Winnie Laverock, a veesitor from East the Coast. She's as bonnie and lively as a robin, and is briskin' up, they say, to Mr Stocks. But, my word, she'll no nab him withoot a warstle. Dae ye see that cummer in black, for a' the warld like a howdie craw wi' a sair gaby? That's Magdalen Jaap, the maister's cousin, but awfu' anxious to be the maister's wife."

Miss Winnie Laverock, whose appearance and character have thus been touched off by the irrepressible Peg, was the daughter of the minister of Pitlochie. Her father was a man of great accomplishments and strong character. Winnie was all that was left of his family; and it was his ambition to teach her everything he knew. And most amply was he repaid for his trouble. She had a merry heart, and a keen and active mind; took an interest in everything; and mastered every subject. Ill-natured people, it is true, sometimes said that "if she was quick to learn, she was also quick to show off." But, as her father remarked, why should her intelligence be kept to herself? If she was witty, how could she help expressing her wit? She was a real gem, and it was her nature to sparkle even amid the dullest surroundings. If there was a ray of light to be got under the whole horizon, she was sure to catch it and reflect it.

As they entered the harvest field, Winnie was in high spirits and full talk. "How delightful this is," she said. "What a glow from the hawthorn hedges and from the ripe grain! I actually feel myself getting warmer and brighter every minute."

"Not brighter," said Mr Stocks, "that would not be possible."

"No irony, Mr Stocks!" she replied. "But here comes Collie to welcome us and do the honours of the field."

"Collie," said Mr Stocks, "is an important personage here. He fancies that he is superintending the shearers."

"Superintending the universe, I should say," replied Miss Laverock, "judging from the way he looks above and around. Controlling the laws of gravity! In fact, he is gravity itself. But, Mr Tosh! why does he put out his tongue, as he stands staring at you?"

"Bad manners, I suppose," said Mr Tosh.

"No," replied Miss Laverock, "he takes you

for the family doctor, and wants you to prescribe."

"Then," said Mr Tosh, "I shall prescribe a little more *bark*."

"Oh, Mr Tosh!" said Miss Laverock. "But what a delightful scene this is! The sight of the shearers with their bright faces and strong arms, the clatter of their sickles, and the rustle of the falling corn, have a strange effect upon me. I feel inclined to share their work. Such is the influence of good example."

"It's like the measles, infectious," said Mr Stocks.

"Or like the moral leaven," replied Miss Laverock, "which leaveneth the whole lump. But I am really ashamed to stand idle before all these industrious people. They must have a low opinion of us. Look at the glances which that stout woman in the striped shortgown is casting at us! She evidently pities me as a poor feckless idler, and thanks Providence that she has got a pair of strong arms and plenty of honest work to do."

"That's Peg Jackson," said Mr Stocks, "the randy of the parish; and I don't think that she is much given to thank Providence for anything."

"Oh," said Miss Laverock, "I don't know. I

should say that she belongs to the sect of the muscular Christians. And she really looks a good all round woman."

"She goes by the nickname of The Bummer," explained Mr Stocks.

"That means the Queen Bee," said Miss Laverock; "and a very appropriate name, for she has got a fine swarm of busy bees around her. But look at that big black man in tattered attire! What an illustration of Shakespeare's phrase, 'looped and windowed raggedness.'"

"Yes," remarked Mr Stocks. "In one way at least he attends to ventilation."

"But," exclaimed Mr Tosh, "what a villainous look he has! That means murder, robbery, and all the other seven deadly sins."

"Not at all," said Miss Laverock. "These black beetle brows were very likely handed down to him from his grandmother, along with a stocking full of her savings. The stocking he has squandered; but he couldn't get rid of the beetle brows."

"Yes," remarked Mr Tosh, "he has squandered the stocking, if we may judge from the bare toes peeping out from the ventilating holes in his shoes."

"That little man beside him," said Mr Stocks, "is his inseparable companion, although he looks a being of a different stamp. He has not been used to this kind of labour. His features are refined, and his hands are white and delicate."

"Oh!" said Mr Tosh, "he's the worst of the two. He reminds me of a portrait I once saw of Jack Sheppard—keen, rat-like eyes, and fingers like claws itching to clutch his prey. But, look! how he is darting glances at Miss Laverock. By Jove, Miss Laverock, you have made a conquest! I congratulate you."

But Miss Laverock did not reply. She was dumb with amazement and horror. The sight of that face had recalled a painful episode in her life; and, under the coarse guise of a reaper, she had recognised one who had formerly been very dear to her. After a few moments she recovered so far, and tried to resume the conversation; but her spirit and elasticity were gone. All the members of her party noticed the sudden collapse. Mr Tosh asked if she had been hurt by the rude staring of that man, and offered to give the fellow a wigging on the spot. And Mr Stocks, remarking that the heat was too much for her, drew her arm into his, and suggested that they should all return to the house.

But there was one person who did not take such a lenient view of the incident. This was Miss Jaap. She had already expressed to her chosen confidante, the tablemaid, her opinion of Miss Laverock.

"People," she had said, "admire what they call her brightness. Well, forwardness is often mistaken for cleverness. I might even use a stronger word than forwardness. I might call it by the good old-fashioned name of impudence. And the way she ogles men, and jokes with them, and leads them on to make idiots of themselves—it's disreputable. That's what it is."

And now, here was an incident which seemed to justify all Miss Jaap's suspicions, and to give her an opportunity of supplanting her rival. Her excitement was so great that she could scarcely walk home quietly along with the others. And when she reached the farm-house, she rushed, bursting with confidence, to the tablemaid.

"Oh, Kirsten!" she cried, "such a scandal to happen in any respectable community! Ye may well cry, 'What is't?' Your precious Miss Laverock exchanging glances with a common shearer on the harvest field, and turning deadly pale. Yes! a common dirty shearer! Some poor unfortunate wretch with whom she has had an intrigue! That woman would intrigue with anything in the shape of a man. You must help me to find out more about him. He is the companion of Black Morgan. I'll expose her; and I'll see that your poor deluded master's eyes are opened."

Talk about vivisection! There are human beings who are vivisected by their fellow-creatures, sometimes consciously, sometimes unconsciously. That day at dinner, Miss Winnie Laverock was one of these hapless victims. The operators were Miss Thomasina Stocks and Mr Tosh; and Miss Jaap, with her bold black eyes, was a keen and gratified spectator of the operation.

First, Miss Stocks insisted upon leading back the conversation to the incident in the harvest field, and again and again expressed her astonishment at Winnie's sudden faintness. "What was it made you ill, I wonder? Was it the heat, do you think? For, you know, you were so well and bright a minute before."

Then Mr Tosh, in turn, after his headlong, haphazard manner, took up the subject. He had, he said, been instituting inquiries about that ruffian who insulted Miss Laverock and made her ill. The fellow, it seemed, called himself Riley, for the nonce at least. Whether it was his real name was very doubtful. Blackguards kept several names, just as decent folks kept several changes of garments, and as soon as one became too soiled, they put on another. Riley was the inseparable pal of Black Morgan, who had the words "burglar" and "garrotter" written on his countenance—yes, written in the Devil's own handwriting. Altogether, this Riley was a bad lot; and those keen eyes and greedy hands must have been inherited from a long line of thieves. He was some desperate criminal in disguise. What if he should turn out to be Crouch, the Glasgow murderer, that they were searching for everywhere?

Under this ruthless talk, poor Miss Laverock sat wincing and quivering and answering at random. At length her host interfered for her relief; and oh! how she thanked him inwardly from the bottom of her heart. Mr Stocks was, what I may be allowed to call, a natural Christian—one who had an instinctive sympathy and consideration for the sufferings of his fellow-creatures. Without the slightest fuss he adroitly diverted the conversation, by asking if they had heard of the last escapade of Rory Brand, the converted shoemaker: and then he told a most ludicrous incident,—how Rory had been at July Fair on an evangelising mission; how, when he was returning in the gloaming, near Inverarden, he had met a shabby old man, apparently a tramp; how he had addressed him at once as a lost sheep, exhorting him to give up his wandering and lawless life; how he had pressed upon him a tract entitled "Hoary Sinner, Stop!" and how this hoary sinner had turned out to be the saintly Dr Gowans, an ex-Moderator, and Convener of the Church's Missionary Society. In this way the attention of the company was diverted from Miss Laverock, and during the remainder of the dinner she was left in comparative peace.

But after she had retired from the table to her own room, she could not rest. She must see this infatuated young man, and ascertain the reason of his extraordinary condition, and implore him to spare her. The proceeding was dangerous, but at all hazards it must be done. So, without more consideration, she put on her hat and went out.

When Miss Laverock passed through the

farmyard, the shearers had emptied their large basins of oatmeal porridge, and were lapped in that most delicious of all luxuries—rest after a long day of hard labour. On the heap of fragrant grass at the stable door reclined three or four Highlanders, passing the snuff-mull, and exchanging their rather stinted sentiments in their native Gaelic. On a seat improvised by the laying of a plank on two upright stones, sat some pawky Aberdonians enveloped in a small cloud of tobacco fumes. And outside on the road, under a tree, was a group of women, mending their linen as they rested their weary limbs on the cool green turf. On another occasion, Winnie's quick sympathy would have enabled her to appreciate this picture of honest well-earned content. But now, her eyes were searching right and left for one figure; and there he was, seated on a stone opposite the garden gate, and attended by his evil genius, Black Morgan. As she passed him, she gave him a glance, which he understood, for he rose and followed her; and when she had walked a short distance, she turned round, and the two stood face to face, ready for an explanation.

But there seemed to be no chance of the

poor girl escaping from her perplexity. She had only time to ask—"Why do you come here, of all places, to disgrace me?" and he had only time to answer—"Don't be alarmed; I shall not disgrace you," when out from the farmyard appeared Mr Stocks, talking with his grieve. Like one surprised in a criminal act, Winnie turned aside abruptly into the garden gate. And there inside the wall was Miss Jaap, who made no attempt to conceal the fact that she had been eaves-dropping. With an air of the most righteous indignation she said,—

"Really, Miss Laverock, for the sake of public decency, you should not be seen talking to that man." And then she went out of the garden into the road as if to get hold of Riley and question him.

"How dare you!" was all that poor Winnie could answer, and then escaped hurriedly to her own room. There her vexation found vent in a tempest of tears and bemoanings.

"Oh, why," she sobbed, "has this happened just when I was so happy, and everything was going so well. And what will Mr Stocks think? I'm anxious to stand well in his opinion. I have such a sincere admiration for him. He is not a genius, but he is something far better—a large-hearted, shrewd-minded man, who cannot fail in any of the duties of life. And to-day, I have liked him more than ever, for the tender and clever way he protected me from these babbling fools. And he is really beginning to show that he likes me. Oh, it is provoking that this hapless ne'er-do-well should turn up here of all places in the world to spoil everything. What should I do? What should I do? Should I run away home at once? No! that would draw more attention to the unfortunate circumstance; and besides, the evil is already done. No! there is another course, a very disagreeable one; but I will face it. Why should I not? Why should I not confess the whole thing to Mr Stocks? He will place himself in my position; and may not think a bit the worse of me. My mind is now made up. In the morning, after breakfast, I shall explain the whole matter to him."

In the morning, however, she did not see Mr Stocks. He had been summoned away to meet the factor on important business, and would not be home till the evening. Her heart sank within her; and she felt that she would never get through the long weary hours. And her misery was intensified by the contrast which she saw in everything around her. There was merriment, as well as excitement, in every countenance. It was to be the last day of harvest, and the great question was, who was to get "the maiden," that is, the last handful of grain that was reaped. To determine this, it is true, a well-known device was generally practised. Some of the young men conspired, before the end of the field was reached, to leave a shock of grain uncut and cover it up with a stook. Then when the close came, and every ear of corn apparently was reaped, the favoured lass was taken to the spot, the stook was cleared away revealing the unreaped shock, she cut it and thus secured "the maiden," and became "the Queen of the Harvest"; but this device required to be cleverly carried out in order to be successful.

Meanwhile, Miss Laverock was passing the weary hours under a cloud of apprehension. Some great calamity, she feared, awaited her. What shape it was to take she could not divine, but it was in some way connected with that unfortunate young man. And when, in the afternoon, she walked out with Miss Stocks and Mr Tosh to see the end of the harvest, she felt as if she were going to her doom. Accordingly, she was not surprised, when, in approaching the Five Acre Park, they became aware of a great hubbub. The end of the harvest had evidently been reached; the reapers were clustering together in a noisy mob at the end of the field; groans mingled with shouts arose in the air; and prominent in the turmoil were seen the figures of Peg Jackson and Black Morgan. "Now," thought Winnie, "it has come at last. My disgrace has been discovered, and will now be held up before the world."

But on this occasion, at least, she was alarming herself needlessly. The commotion was caused by no serious matter. Peg Jackson, it seems, at the dinner hour had noticed three or four stalks of corn that had been left uncut by the side of the field. She had squatted down upon them, and had beaten them flat, and concealed them under her capacious person; and as she was always the first to sit down and the last to rise up, no one had seen them. She waited till the device for securing "the maiden," which we have explained above, was carried out, and Grace

Fleming, the favoured damsel, was proclaimed "the Harvest Queen."

Then she came forward and protested that the last of the harvest was not yet reaped; and in proof of the statement she went to the handful of grain which she had concealed in such a grotesque way, cut it, and held it up in triumph. Many loudly demurred; but others declared that The Bummer was right, that she had got "the maiden," and a proposition was made to carry her shoulder high. Peg, however, was not to be trifled with; and when Black Morgan advanced to lay hold of her, she gave him a cuff which sent him backwards into a stook.

This cloud of alarm melted away without doing any damage; but a more ominous one was gathering on the horizon. That evening, the shearers were to be entertained in the barn to a supper and a dance; and the farmer and his friends were expected to be present at a part of the entertainment. At eight o'clock, the ladies were in their rooms making ready to go into the barn, when a cry arose, that Miss Stocks's jewel-case was stolen. The last time it had been seen was at the dinner hour of the previous day. Mr Stocks, who had just arrived from his journey, summoned the whole household—guests, servants, and all—to ascertain if any clue could be got to the mystery. No one could give any definite information. Then Miss Jaap, who, it was evident to all, was bursting with something, struck in:—

"It's that man Riley. He was hanging about the garden gate last night. You saw him, Miss Laverock, and you were speaking to him; and, by the by, you must have left the garden door of the house ajar, for it was found open this morning, and that was the way by which the thief must have got in. And what confirms his guilt is, that he has disappeared. He wasn't at his work to-day. Do you know where he is, Miss Laverock?"

"Magdalen," said Mr Stocks sternly, "there must be no rash accusations. What we have got to do is not to suspect, but to detect. I shall wait till to-morrow morning, and if the matter is not cleared up by that time, it must be put into the hands of the police. Meantime, Magdalen, don't introduce Miss Laverock's name. She has got nothing to do with it: depend upon that."

What Miss Laverock's feelings were during

this ordeal may be imagined but can't be described. When it was all over, the only remark that she could make was, that she could not go to see the shearers. But Miss Stocks, taking her aside, and kissing and coaxing her, said, "Don't mind what that spiteful cat insinuates. It is all jealousy. Show your contempt for her by appearing as usual, and going about as usual." And Winnie set out with her friend to the barn.

When they reached the barn, the supper was over, and the tables and forms were being cleared away to make room for the dance. Whether it was owing to the solid nature of the viands, or to a scanty supply of inspiriting beverage, I can't say, but the men and women were dull and dumb, and the sight of their betters from the big house only tended to make them look more sheepish and awkward. How they were to be entertained seemed to be a great difficulty. But a remedy was at hand.

There was present an Orpheus who could animate the stocks and the stones. This was the old, bandy-legged fiddler, Geordie Wilkie. On ordinary occasions he was a simple clod-hopper, trudging at the plough tail, or sitting upon his muddy cart; but at a foy, a penny wedding, or any other merrymaking, he was a potentate, a magician swaying the crowds at will, as the moon sways the waters of the deep. On this particular night, he was, as he himself expressed it, "in fine fettle." No sooner did he, after a few preliminary tunings and squeakings, strike up an old-fashioned reel, than the dead mass of humanity began to move, and throb, and leap. The music, like electricity, had flashed through their nerves and muscles and made them jump into life. In a trice they had fallen into sets and were involved in the mazes of the dance, thumping the floor with their hob-nailed shoes, cracking their horny fingers, grinning and grimacing to their partners, "hooching," and wheeling nimbly about, shaking off their cares as a dog shakes off the hail-drops, and looking as if there was to be no more worry or want in this world, and all was to be peace and plenty for evermore.

On another occasion, Winnie, with her sunny sympathetic disposition, would have entered thoroughly into this scene, and would have enjoyed to the full all its escapades and humours. But now her heart was frozen by despair, and could not feel anything like pleasure. Their bright merriment by its contrast only made her despondency all the darker. It seemed a mockery of her grief, and aggravated it intensely. She looked on in agony, and was wondering where she should go and what she should do, when she saw the unwonted sight of a policeman at the door of the barn; and immediately afterwards a servant whispered in her ear, "Please, Miss, you are wanted in the parlour." Then she knew that the catastrophe was at hand, and went away to meet it.

But a strange change had come over her—a change which surprised herself. Despair had become desperation, and she now felt herself perfectly calm and collected. She was eager to make a full explanation of the whole matter, and to abide the consequences. Therefore, when she entered the parlour, and saw a policeman, with the official calmness on his countenance, and Riley well dressed and bright, and Mr Stocks anxious and perplexed, and Miss Jaap flushed and giving her evidence, she was not surprised, but quietly took a seat and listened.

Miss Jaap in excited tones was telling her story—how she had seen Riley last night about seven o'clock watching the garden gate, how she had gone back half an hour afterwards and found him still lurking there, and how she was sure it was he who took the jewels, and it could be no one else. Then turning to Winnie, she said, "You know that this is true, Miss Laverock, for you saw him and were talking to him on the road, and came in through the garden and did not lock the door, and that was the way he got into the house."

At this venomous speech the hearers were visibly fluttered. Mr Stocks looked stern indignation; the policeman condescended to smile contemptuously; and Riley, producing a box, asked Miss Jaap if that was the stolen article.

"Ah, look there now!" cried Miss Jaap; "was I not right? He's obliged to confess that he is the thief."

"No, Miss! there you are wrong. But," he added, after listening to footsteps coming along the passage, "here, if I mistake not, comes the thief."

And two policemen entered with Black Morgan in charge.

"So," growled out Morgan, regarding Riley with a murderous look, "you hound, you split upon your pal after all your gammon! But look here, policemen, this smaik is the real boss of the plant. He has got the jewel-case on him."

" Right so far," replied Riley coolly; " but I took it from you in the way of business. I am Macnab, the detective."

" The d—— you are," exclaimed Morgan. " Whew —— by ——, if I had known that, I would have spoilt your mug for you. Mean! low! mean! d——d mean!"

"Come now, Morgan," said Riley, "don't be uncharitable. Every man to his trade. Your trade is wholesale criminal. Mine is detective officer. You prosecuted yours with unflagging enthusiasm. Allow me to do the same. I was asked to look after you. From information received you were thought to be the man wanted for a notorious crime. It was a difficult job, for you were up to no end of dodges. Now, I had always been fond of play-acting. In fact, I was once upon the boards. So I resolved to dress up as a brother pal, and I stuck to you like a brother and followed you here. And you must confess that I made up and performed the part to perfection. And what's more, I have got the evidence that I wanted. You are not Will Morgan. You know you are not. You are

James Crouch, that has been wanted so long for the Trongate murder."

This intelligence startled the little company like the shock of an earthquake. The thought that they were in the presence of that ruthless cut-throat, Crouch, who for so many weeks had been advertised for and sought for all over the country, and also in the presence of Macnab, the famous Glasgow detective, produced what journalists call "a sensation." For several minutes they could do nothing but devour with their eyes the criminal, who returned their stare with a scowl of defiance. But their amazement was interrupted by the detective and the policemen rising and preparing to leave with their charge. While doing so, the detective glanced at Miss Laverock, and said, "I'll call here and see you to-morrow morning."

The company in the parlour sat for some time expressing their astonishment at this wonderful denouement. Then Winnie, noticing that Miss Jaap still regarded her with suspicion, fairly turned on her.

"You are wondering, Miss Jaap, what connection this detective has with me. Well! I shall tell you. This man is *not* my husband. He is not even my discarded lover, a statement which you were overheard making to Kirsten the tablemaid. He is only my brother, nothing more. He was an only son, and my father devoted his whole time to his education, and resolved to make him a scholar. But when Eric (that's my brother's name, and his middle name is Macnab) was ready for the University, he refused to go. He said that he had no taste for learning, and that his whole heart was for acting, and that he would go upon the stage. Now, my father is passionate, imperious, and accustomed to get his own way. Besides, if there is one calling that he considers disreputable it is *play-acting*, as he styles it. He therefore solemnly declared that if Eric went upon the stage, he would from that moment disinherit and disown him. But Eric, who had inherited his father's hot and wilful temper, declared that he would not be forced into a profession which he hated, that he himself was the best judge of what he was best fitted for, and that if his own father chose to throw him off, he would fend for himself. So he went away and disappeared; and for years, up till yesterday in fact, we have seen and heard nothing of him. Now, Miss Jaap, was it not natural that

I should be disturbed when I came unexpectedly on my long-lost brother in the harvest field? Was it not natural that I should blush for him, when I saw him in the garments of a hireling reaper? And was it not natural that I should try to have a talk with him? And was it not very cruel, Miss Jaap, when you had only these grounds to go upon, to jump to the conclusion that I was an abandoned girl, and actually to accuse me of aiding and abetting in this robbery of the jewel-case? I ask you, Miss Jaap, has your conduct not been very, very cruel?"

Miss Jaap sat silent, and only replied by a look of inveterate hatred.

But Mr Stocks, in the most earnest manner said, "If nobody else will reply, I will, Miss Laverock. You have been used most cruelly. You were invited to the house as a guest, and you have been treated like a criminal. As the master of the house I humbly apologise; and as for Miss Jaap, she ought to go down on her knees and ask your pardon for her vile suspicions and accusations."

But this only brought Miss Jaap's hate to a climax, for she rose up in stern silence and went out of the room.

"That woman's unamiability," said Mr Stocks, "is a most pitiable spectacle. She was always irritable; but latterly her bad temper has become chronic. It is a madness, a monomania, which she takes a morbid pleasure in nursing. Almost every person is looked upon as an enemy, and almost every act as an insult. I myself am afraid to move or to speak lest I offend her. But I will stand it no longer. She shall go at once. I have done with her."

"Don't, Mr Stocks, I entreat you, cast her off," said Miss Laverock. "You are her only friend, I understand. The poor thing is more to be pitied than blamed. Her infirmity is more physical than moral. It is the result of biliousness, and can only be cured by medical treatment. But I believe that I am partly to blame. My presence and my incessant chatter have aggravated her. I know that I talk too much. Ever since I was a child, my father has made me his companion, and has encouraged me to give my opinion on every subject; and when in company, I am apt to forget that other people are not so partial as he is, and I allow my tongue to go like a bell. And poor Miss Jaap, along with others, has suffered. My everlasting gabble must be a great nuisance."

"Well!" replied Mr Stocks, "if that's gabble, then all I have to say is that I don't wish to hear anything better than gabble during the rest of my life."

"There's no accounting for taste," said Winnie laughing. "But, Mr Stocks, to speak seriously, you'll not cast that poor thing off? Remember that you are her best friend. If you do, I shall be very miserable, for I shall feel that I have been the cause of it. You'll not do it, will you?"

"Well, Miss Laverock, if it's to give you pain, I will not do it."

"Now! that's like you. And you'll find that everything will now go right. I'm going home to-morrow, and Miss Jaap will then become quiet. This (*pointing to her jacket*) is the red rag that has made the cow mad. When this is removed the cow will settle down to chew the cud—yes, the cud of sweet and bitter memories."

Mr Stocks was now aghast. "Miss Laverock," he stammered, "you can't mean it. No, no—it will never do—why, you have only been here two days, and you came to stay a month at least. I was looking forward—that is, *we* were all looking forward—to a happy time, and now"—and here the good man's feelings overpowered him, and fairly carried him away. What he said he never could exactly remember; but he gave her to understand that he could not do without her, and that, deprived of her presence, life would not be worth living.

Then she, blushing very much, yet unable to repress a merry twinkle in her eye, said that this was dreadful. It was just another proof that she had been too long there. She was the wicked fairy that, without meaning it, had introduced confusion into the family. She must, however, persist in going home to-morrow. She wished to be present at the meeting between her father and brother, and to try to reconcile them. But (*and here she looked down and faltered in her speech*) if her father approved, and she had no doubt he would, she would come back; and after all the proper forms had been gone through she would stay. She could not bear the idea of having his death upon her conscience, or even his unhappiness—all the more so as she had always admired and liked him, especially during her late trouble, when he had shown her so much sympathy and good feeling. Would he agree to this arrangement?

Of course, he was only too delighted to agree; and he was anxious that there should be witnesses to the agreement. So he led her into the drawing-room, where Miss Stocks and Miss Jaap were sitting, and introduced her as his affianced bride. Miss Stocks rushed to her, and took her in her arms; Miss Jaap bounced out of the room.

"What wonderful chemical properties I must have," said Winnie. "I possess the power both of attraction and repulsion."

"No wonder," said Mr Stocks, "that she is ashamed to look you in the face, after accusing you of theft."

"But," said Winnie, "I was really guilty of theft. I stole your heart; but you punished me, for you stole mine."

THE BOY HERETIC.

THE parish of Sandyriggs had been, time out of mind, noted for its orthodoxy. In the days of the Covenant its inhabitants had suffered for the good cause; and at the Battle of Tippermuir its most prominent men had sealed their testimony with their blood. It had also been blessed with a long succession of faithful ministers, both Established and Seceding, men who had not only held the form of sound doctrine, but also of sound words. The minister of the parish, at this time, was the Rev. Jeremiah MacGuffog, a preacher famous all over the land for his persistent and deadly attacks upon organs, images, printed prayers, human hymns, private interpretations of Scripture, intemperance, and all the other backslidings of the day. The result was, that while heresy was breaking out in various parts of the country, it never was known in Sandyriggs. The theological atmosphere was evidently too keen and bracing for such a hothouse plant.

Imagine, then, the sensation when it was reported that, at last, heresy had appeared among the rising generation. The inhabitants were struck dumb at first; but gradually recovering themselves, they began to talk about it. It was discussed by the men at the church door on Sunday, and by the women over their *four hours* tea. What could be the cause of it, was a question frequently asked? One suggested bad education; while another asserted that it was too much education, and boldly wished for the return of the good old time when the young bolted their knowledge as they bolted their monthly dose of castor oil, and never thought of complaining that it disagreed with them.

The *fama clamosa* became so great that it could no longer be ignored in his pulpit messages by that faithful minister, the Rev. Mr MacGuffog. With bated breath he told his hearers that this was only one instance among many of the fact that the spirit of evil had rallied his powers and was making a desperate attempt to ruin mankind. "Yet," he added, "this incident which has taken place in our midst is also fraught with comfort; because it is the fulfilment of the prophecy that children will rise up against their parents; and, taken with the wars and rumours of wars that prevail in the world at present, it is a sign that the glorious time is at hand when Satan shall be bound for a thousand years."

Who was this arch heretic, this chosen emissary of Satan, at whom the parish turned pale? Little Willie Torrance, aged seven, the son of George Torrance, a small farmer. What were the influences under which this heresy was developed, it is now our task to describe.

Willie was what his mother called "a fell laddie," and his father "a fair heartbreak." Do what they liked, they could never make him behave like other boys. His dull red hair was always in disorder; his face seemed a favourite resting-place for dust and smut; his hands were soiled with the stroking of rabbits and pigeons; and his corduroys were torn and worn with the climbing of trees. A book was a thing which he never of his own accord touched. When he should have been learning his lessons, he was outside watching the ducklings and the chicks; and on Sabbath evenings, when all the members of the family were questioned on the Shorter Catechism, he mixed up the answers in the most profane and ludicrous manner. Every effort was tried to reclaim him. His brother and sister, who were much older than he, were most faithful in holding up before him all his sins against cleanliness and order; his father at intervals conscientiously applied Solomon's educative instrument, the rod; and his mother, though longing to be kind and sympathetic, frowned upon many of his ways. But all these measures seemed to produce no effect. He, indeed, endured all their treatment without a murmur or protest, and really felt at times that he was a bad lot and would come to a bad end; but his patience was unhesitatingly pronounced to be "dourness," and was added on to his list of crimes.

But in spite of all this, he could not have been a bad boy, for he had some devoted friends. The moment he appeared in the farmyard, his presence was hailed by both "the fowl and the brute." In the sound of his voice and the touch of his hand there was that miraculous power, sympathy, which at once won their hearts. He understood them and they understood him. Sweep, the cat, rubbed and purred against his leg; Rover, the dog, jumped up to kiss his face; Blaze, the bob-tailed horse, turned round its head in its stall to neigh to him; the brown calf put its nose over the fence to be scratched; and the pigeons settled on him like a small cloud to eat the corn from his hand.

But Willie's greatest blessing was his staunch bosom friend, Bob Fortune. A friend is dear at any time, but he is especially dear in our childhood, when the heart is fresh, the conscience clean, and the world full of untasted pleasures. Not only is he another self, doubling our delights and lessening our troubles, but he is what Shakespeare calls "an earth-treading star," shedding a new light on everything. Answering exactly to this description was Bob Fortune, nine years of age, and a neighbour farmer's son, who called in, every morning, for Willie and accompanied him to school. He was a healthy, hearty, intelligent boy. It seemed as if his soul were made of sunlight, which warmed every limb and shone through every feature. He had a smile and a soft word for every living creature; and it was only when he witnessed cruelty that he was ever out of temper. Overflowing, too, with animal spirits and all kinds of boyish accomplishments, he was ever ready to run, leap, sing, whistle, and imitate all sorts of sounds. He was also clever with his hands and with his tongue, and, therefore, well fitted to be not only a friend but a protector to Willie.

Your ordinary boy is apt to be cruel. He is as Dickens remarks, "an enemy to all creation." He stones cats, beats the dumb driven cattle, robs birds' nests, and in general gets "his sport," as he calls it, at the expense of the lower animals. Like his full-grown fellow-sportsmen, when he wants to be happy, he says, "Let us go and kill something." This habit is not the result, as some suppose, of the cruelty inherent in human nature, but rather arises from sheer thoughtlessness. It never occurs to him that the lower animals feel the same pain as we do; and, strange as it may seem, in this age of education, sympathy towards our fellow-creatures is not taught at school.

From this savage habit our two lads had been saved by a painful accident. One day a pretty, bright, playful young spaniel, named Spring, which they had just been fondling, darted before a carriage, and was run over and killed. Willie, especially, was dreadfully shocked, and could not get rid of the sight of the poor animal writhing in the death throes on the hard road, looking up pitifully into his face as if struggling to tell what it was suffering, and venting all its agony in one long, pitiful whine. Next day he stated to Bob that it was wrong to torment animals, "for," he said, "they suffer jist like hiz." They both resolved that they would not be cruel to any creature, and that they would no longer rob nests. They might take one egg, but that would not matter, as the bird could not count and would never miss it. Then they wondered where Spring was now; and Bob, whose imagination was always active, declared that he was sure to be in heaven. Good dogs, he said, must go to heaven; for their masters, when they went there, could not be happy without them. To Willie this reasoning was conclusive, for he could not fancy any perfect state of happiness where there were no four-footed favourites.

Our story begins on a bright summer morning, when the two boys set out together for school. Delightful as their walks always were, this particular walk was to be more delightful than usual. They had scarcely left the farm buildings and were passing a whinny knowe, when out there came running in a great state of flutter and anger, as if to attack them, a hen partridge. Knowing by this that her brood was near, they searched among the furze, and found instead of young partridges, five barn-door chickens. There they were—yellow, black, and white—staggering on their wire-like legs, and wondering very much at this strange world into which they had evidently just newly come. On searching still further, they came upon a nest with the empty shells. It was evident that the pair of partridges, having been robbed of their own eggs, had come upon this neglected nest, had taken possession of it, had hatched the brood and were now trying, like good foster-parents, to bring up their adopted family.

The next object before which the boys stood was a well-grown larch at the foot of the avenue. On it was their favourite nest, a chaffinch's, a perfect specimen of bird-craft. They had been able to examine and admire it by climbing a neighbouring tree and looking into it. It was snugly and securely placed in a fork of the larch, was cosy inside with hair, wool, and feathers, and outside was covered skilfully all over with lichen so as to look like a bit of the tree. They had also taken an interest in the two birds, and by feeding them every day with seed had made them quite tame. On this morning, the boys saw that something unusual had happened; for the hen-bird was flitting excitedly between the ground and the nest, and the cock was singing his favourite song with more than his usual briskness; and on climbing the neighbouring tree, they saw that the nest was full of gaping little bills. No wonder that the mother was busy and the father proud!

But the most exciting event was seen when they were passing along the pathway that skirts the back of the Gibbet Wood. Out in the air above the field, a beak-and-claw fight was going on between two birds that were discovered to be a wood-pigeon and a sparrow-hawk. The pigeon was having the worst of it, and its feathers were falling fast, when some crows, happening to pass, darted upon the common foe, the hawk, and forced it to let go its hold. The pigeon alighted on a wall to recover itself and then disappeared, and the hawk retreated, pursued and harassed by its black enemies.

Then without further adventures they sauntered along by the loch side under the blue unclouded weather. Bright and sympathetic, they formed a part of the general joy that was abroad on the earth. They carolled with the lark, whistled with the blackbird, and sported with the butterfly among the flowers. And in the intervals Bob, full of bright fancies, told what he was to do when he was a man: how he was going to be a farmer, and have a garden full of the bonniest flowers, and keep all kinds of horses, dogs, rabbits, and birds.

But when the boys reached the village and looked down the Overgate where the school was situated, a sudden change came over their mood. There was a dreadful silence which struck terror into them. The school "was in" and they would be punished for being late. With fluttering hearts they mounted the outside stair, went through the " pend " that led to the school building, opened the door, stood before the indignant teacher and the expectant and by no means sympathetic scholars, took their punishment bravely, and sat down with smarting hands to their work.

This humble institution was about the last specimen of its class. It was an instance of the comparative ease with which, not so long ago, schools could be set up, and schoolmasters could be made. The schoolmaster, Mr Sloan, had been a house-carpenter. When old age began to steal upon him, and he found manual labour too much for his strength, he was advised by his fellow-elders in the small sect to which he belonged to start a school. "You've a gude haund o' write," they said, "and ye're no a bad coonter; and the members o' oor body will send their bairns to ye." He took their advice, and carried it out with the greatest ease. First of all, there was no difficulty about getting a schoolroom. Choosing his own workshop, he cleared out the benches and the shavings, scrubbed the earthen floor, swept down the bare walls, put in a few plain desks and forms which he had made with his own hand; and the thing was done. According to his idea, no more furnishings, such as maps, globes, or pictures, were required. Then there was just as little difficulty in converting himself into a schoolmaster. He laid aside his working-man's clothes, wore his Sunday best every day, bought a bit of old leather and fashioned it into *tawse;* and lo! the transformation was complete. The housecarpenter in one day had been changed into a teacher of youth.

Equally simple and easy was his method of

education. All he required his pupils to do, besides their writing and arithmetic, was to commit to memory the Shorter Catechism, Proofs, and Psalms; and he rested satisfied that these good words, when swallowed, like a blessed medicine would purify the heart, and enlighten the head. And all that he, the teacher, needed to do was to direct and stimulate them by means of the tawse; for did not the wise man say that the scourge was the great instrument to be used in the education of the young! "He that spareth the rod hateth the child." His scholars were placed on the plain, beaten highway, and his whole duty was to drive them forward. He was an educational *drover*. He was never known to have given a single explanation of any kind on any subject whatever.

On this particular day, it chanced that the work of the school bore very hard on poor Willie Torrance. The first lesson he was called upon to say was a question in the Shorter Catechism. "Wherein," asked the teacher, in slow and solemn tones, "consists the sinfulness of that estate whereinto man fell?" "The sinfulness," answered Willie, in a lugubrious, sing-song voice, "of that estate whereinto man fell"

—and then he came to a dead stop. "Go on, sir!" said the teacher, sternly. Willie could only run over again, "The sinfulness," etc., in the desperate hope that he would thus gain an impetus which would carry him through the remainder of the answer; but it was all in vain. Leather was applied smartly to the palm of his hand; but this, while it gave a keener realisation of the *feeling* of the sinfulness, did not contribute at all to its *theological conception*. He was sent to his seat in disgrace, and sentenced to be kept in during the dinner-hour to learn his neglected task.

The reading lesson came next, and every boy and girl was called upon in turn to read a verse. The chapter was in the Old Testament, and consisted chiefly of a long list of jaw-twisting Hebrew names. Easy-going teachers used to skip such a chapter,—one of them, an irreverent Gallio, alleging as a reason, that it was "a mere hatteril o' nick-names." But Mr Sloan, a strictly orthodox man, held that every word and letter, nay, every jot and tittle, were "profitable for instruction in righteousness," and would not tolerate this playing fast and loose with the inspired record. As it was, these Jewish names stuck in Willie's throat. In the supple jaws of old Orientals, without doubt, they were as a sweet morsel to be rolled under the tongue; but, in the narrow and stiff jaws of a Scotch boy, they were hard nuts which could neither be cracked nor swallowed. A smart box on the ear was suddenly administered, but it did not contribute to the clearing of the head, or the loosening of the vocal organs. There was no help for the lad. He was left in the midst of the verse, like a lamb entangled in a thicket of brambles, and the class proceeded with the remainder of the task.

The writing lesson followed. Willie, grasping the pen tightly between the forefinger and thumb, dipped it in the ink; but alas! the ink bottle was too full, and, on bringing out the pen, he let a big blot fall upon the paper. He licked the ink up with his tongue; but a very ugly mark was left upon the copy. And when he tried to make a stroke he only made another blot. The master gave him a smart rap on the knuckles with the ruler; but this only shook his hand, and flustered him. He could not keep his fingers free from the black liquid; and, in his desperation, he wiped them sometimes on his corduroys, sometimes on his hair, and sometimes on his face, until he looked as if he had been exposed to a shower of ink.

The dinner-hour now intervened, and he was locked up in the schoolroom all alone to get up the Catechism lesson which he had been unable to repeat. By dint of sheer hammering, he managed to fix the words, not the meaning, in his memory. Yet all the while he was looking out on a green hill opposite, where a boy of his acquaintance was herding a cow. Oh! how he envied that boy! How delightful it would be if he could get free for ever from school, and pass the long summer day in the open air, rolling on the grass among his favourite animals!

After the dinner-hour came the most difficult task of all. A column of figures on the slate was put before him, and he was told to add them up. He did not know how to add; he did not know even the meaning of the word, and no explanation was vouchsafed to him. He sat wondering how it should be done, and feeling that his brain was becoming a mass of confusion. Casting a stealthy glance upon his neighbour's slate, he found that his neighbour was putting down quite easily under the column a row of figures. He concluded that the whole thing was a puzzle, and was only to be found out by experiment. Accordingly, he tried first one set of figures and then another, but every time he was wrong. At last the master, losing patience, was driven to the use of sarcasm. Seizing the boy's ear, twisting him round, and pointing to a stucco bust which was over the door, and which, indeed, was the sole ornament in the school, he said, in withering tones, "There's your brother." Then, tapping the little confused skull, he added, "You've a head, and so has a pin." The whole school laughed at these sarcasms. They were well known. They were the master's only jokes, and, therefore, did duty very often.

Willie had now run the gantlet of all the lessons and all the punishment. The road to knowledge had not been to him a green and flowery lane, along which he was led with ease and delight. It had rather been a thorny brake, through which he had been dragged by main force, and from which he issued hot, dishevelled, and bleeding. It never occurred to him to ask, "What is the use of all this?" He had a vague impression that this education, like measles and whooping cough, was one of those serious dispensations of Providence which all must go through, and which must be borne with patience.

But now came a relief. Mr Sloan, soothed by the good dinner which he had just eaten, sank into his usual afternoon nap; and the scholars immediately turned from their books and slates to subdued fun and talking. Willie, greatly relieved, stood up and began to tell his neighbour, Button Bowie, as they called him, all the strange sights which he and Bob Fortune had seen that morning: the partridge with the brood of chickens, the chaffinch's nest, and the fight between the wood-pigeon and the sparrow-hawk.

But this interval of relief was not to last long. In every school, just as in every company of human beings, there is always to be found a bully; and this bully requires two persons near him,— a victim to be tormented by him, and a toady to laugh at his cleverness. Christopher Bain, nine years of age, was the bully; poor, harmless Willie was the victim; and Button Bowie, whose father was foreman to Bain's father, was the toady. Bain founded his superiority on the fact that his father was the largest farmer in the neighbourhood, and kept a gig. He was conceited, brazen-faced, and loud. Coming forward, he cried, "Weel, what's that little numskull, that dunce o' the hale schule, been sayin' noo? He's gettin' stupider than ever."

Button, eager to curry favour with the son of his father's employer, told him.

"Ye lee'in beggar," said Bain to Willie, as if in righteous indignation, "hoo daur ye tell sic stories? Why, ye're sae stupid that ye wadna ken a pigeon frae a hawk. Ye wadna ken a B from a bull's fit;" and, so saying, he gave the little fellow a push which sent him sprawling on the floor.

While some of the girls cried out "Shame," and Button Bowie sniggered, Bob Fortune exclaimed, "Stop that, ye big coward. Strike ane o' yer ain size. I tell the same story that Willie telt aboot what he saw this mornin'. Ca' me a leer! Try 't!"

"Ay, I'll try 't," retorted Bain in a blustering voice.

"Just try 't," repeated Bob.

"Ay, I'll try 't, and dae't tae."

But now an explosive snore proclaimed that the master was waking, and in an instant the scholars were intent on their slates and books, just as if they had never stopped their studies;

and the teacher himself tried to look as if he had never been asleep, but had only shut his eyes to think out some deep problem. A fine bit of acting on both sides!

After the scholars were dismissed, Bob and Willie went to do some errands at the village shops, and then they took their way homewards. When they came to the foot of the avenue, whom should they see but Bain and Bowie looking up at the chaffinch's nest? "Oh, ho!" cried Bain, "so, this is yer precious nest;" and before they had any idea of what was going to happen, the wretch had shot a stone with unerring aim, and the ruins of the nest and the young birds, gasping out their little lives, were lying on the hard ground. Willie burst into tears; but Bob, rushing at the heartless rascal, thrashed him soundly, and ended by throwing him down in a bed of nettles. Bain, starting up, ran to a distance, and then threw a big stone which, had not Bob smartly ducked, might have done serious damage. Bob, crying out, "Twa can play at that game," sent after him a missile which hit him on the small of the back, and he went howling round the corner, followed by his sympathising spaniel, Button Bowie. Bob and Willie sorrowfully gathered up the murdered birds, and buried them in a tuft of moss, while the parents, fluttering round, filled the air with their distressful notes.

The next day, Thursday, was the annual fast, which, in this primitive village of Sandyriggs, was most rigidly observed. As the preparation for the solemn rites of the communion, it was considered even more sacred than the Sabbath itself. Any secular work or any amusement on such a day was considered to be an act of desecration. There is a story still handed down, that a stranger, who was passing through the village on a Fast Day, and who chanced to whistle, was stoned by the natives, and obliged to run for his life. I myself distinctly remember my horror when I saw two boys on such an occasion playing at marbles. I trembled lest lightning should fall from heaven, and strike them dead. But of late, there were some bold spirits who regarded this day as a mere human institution, and, therefore, not binding upon them. Bob Fortune's father was one of these. On principle, neither he nor his children went to church on a Fast Day. And thus it happened that Bob had told Willie that he was going on the morrow to see his big brother fish in the loch.

P

On the forenoon of the Fast Day, George Torrance, silent and serious, like a man bent on living up to a high ideal, set out with all his family to church. It was a brilliant summer day, and as they went along Willie could not help occasionally giving vent to his delight, when a golden butterfly wavered across his path, or a lark sprang up singing from a neighbouring grass field. But his unseasonable joy was frowned down by his father; and his mother said, "For ony sake, laddie, mind whatna day it is." When they came to the loch, there was Bob Fortune in the distance. He had taken off his shoes, and was lying on his back on the grass, and luxuriating in the sunshine. On seeing them, he rose up and waved to them. Willie had soon good reason for remembering that action. For the rest of his life, the image of the bright boy waving his hand never left his memory.

The services that day in the church, in which George Torrance was an elder, were solemn and long. First of all, the minister of the congregation, Mr Peden, went up into the pulpit, gave out a psalm to be sung, and offered up a long prayer. Then, while a second psalm was being sung, he gave place to a reverend brother, Mr

Herd, of the Byres, who, not satisfied with the prayer already given, thought it necessary to engage in another of equal length. The sermon came next, severely doctrinal, many-headed, long-tailed; and then a short prayer and a psalm concluded the forenoon service. Mr Torrance, in the interval, led his family to a room in a private house, where they silently lunched on *baps* and ale. The afternoon service was a repetition of that of the forenoon, with one of the long prayers left out.

Some people of the present day may be inclined to sneer at this service as "weary, stale, flat, and unprofitable." But to the intelligent and pious rustics who had few books, it was an intellectual and a spiritual treat, which edified and refreshed them. Their most heartfelt associations clustered round the church and its worship, and they could sing with genuine feelings the lines of the psalm:

> "Blessed are they in Thy courts that dwell,
> They ever give Thee praise."

A great mistake, however, was made in subjecting mere children to these ordinances. It was thought, indeed, that the preaching of the Word, though not understood, was bound to touch them and foster within them a love of religion. The very reverse, however, was often the result. Their bodies were wearied out, their minds were stupefied, and they formed disagreeable associations with the church, which were sometimes never dispelled.

Willie Torrance, in the afternoon especially, passed through a very disagreeable ordeal. He sat on a high, hard seat with his feet dangling in the air. Under the influence of the heat of the crowded church, and the monotonous tones of the minister, he fell fast asleep. Then he was roughly awakened by a nudge from his father, and a kick from his brother; and his mother whispered to him, "Sit up, and listen to the minister." The poor lad, rubbing his eyes, tried to obey her, but he could not understand a single scrap of the sermon. It was as meaningless and depressing to him as the moaning of the east wind at the kitchen window on a wild winter night. What could he do, therefore, but sit wearily, and allow his thoughts to stray to all sorts of things, and, above all, wonder what Bob was doing at the loch side, until the word "Amen" told him that the sermon was at last done, and the end of his imprisonment near. What a welcome sound had that word always been! It was the only part of a discourse that ever stirred him; and even in a dead sleep he could hear it, and waken up with the feeling that a wearisome ordeal was passed. Yet on that particular day when he came out into the sunshine, he did not experience his usual joy. A strange depression lay upon his spirits. He could not help feeling that God was angry with him for not listening to the sermon, and for not liking the church. He had also the apprehension that a punishment was hanging over him, and on this occasion that apprehension was fated to be realised.

On their way home, when they came near the loch, he saw that something unusual had happened. A group of people were standing on the bank, and talking excitedly; and two men, hurrying towards the village, whispered something to his father, who was in front. He heard the name, "Fortune," and in another minute he became conscious that a terrible calamity had befallen him. His boy friend and protector was drowned.

Two young men, in the course of the day, had come to the loch, and had got hold of a boat to have a row, and had invited Bob to go along with them. When they were at some distance from the land, the two young men fell into a dispute, and after the foolish manner of gawks, stood up in the boat and had some horse-play. In an instant the boat was upset, and the three occupants were in the water struggling for life. The young men managed, with difficulty, to reach the shore; but the boy, who was not a swimmer, could only cling to the bottom of the boat. For some time he struggled to get out of the water on to the keel, crying desperately all the while for help. But his brother could not swim, and the two young men were either too tired or too timid to venture to rescue him; and while they were standing wondering what they should do, the poor lad, worn out with his ineffectual struggles, sank out of sight. A minute afterwards, men from the neighbouring farm arrived in another boat, but it was too late. All they could do now was to recover the body. After an hour's dragging, it was found, placed on a barn door, and covered with a cloak to be carried home. The Torrances, on arriving at the loch side, saw the melancholy procession proceeding up the road by the Mill Farm.

This terrible disaster fell upon Willie like a blow, and stunned him. His powers were paralysed, and he could neither speak nor weep.

He saw the loch, the excited groups on the shore, and the muffled figure, lying on the barn door, disappearing in the distance; but the whole scene appeared to be a terrible nightmare. This stupor continued as he walked home, and sat silent by the fire. But after he had gone to bed, his mother heard him sobbing, and, in a voice half-choked with tears, praying that God would restore to life his lost friend. And in the morning he was really hopeful that his prayer would be answered. God had raised the dead in past times, and why should He not do the same now? And he actually waited for his daily companion, looking up the pathway in the Back Planting, and expecting to see him, as formerly, coming bounding down like a deer. But he waited and looked in vain, and was obliged to set out for school alone.

As he went along the familiar road, his grief broke out afresh. Almost every object reminded him of his best friend, who was gone, and would never, never come again. He lingered awhile with a strange, melancholy feeling over the ruins of the chaffinch's nest that still lay on the road. There was one object, however, that he could not face, and that was the cruel loch which had drowned his friend; and to escape it he went round by the Myre Farm, and down the links. Then as he came near the village, the thought suddenly flashed across his brain: What if Bob should be there, if he should have recovered, and, for some reason, gone to school by another way, and should be sitting waiting for him? But alas! no such joyful experience awaited him, but another of a very different kind.

There is a set of well-meaning but narrow-minded Christians, who take a very paltry view of God's government of this vast and complicated universe. They imagine that every calamity is a judgment, that it is the punishment of some particular sin, and that this sin can be identified. They are also convinced that it is their duty to call attention to this calamity, and hold it up as a warning to their fellow-men. And this they call "sanctifying the dispensation of Providence." Mr Sloan was one of these; and when Willie entered, he was beginning to read to his awe-struck scholars a speech which his minister, the Rev. Mr Moodie, of the Original Protesting Church, had prepared for him:

"They were met," he said, "under the gloom of a sad calamity. One of their number, while playing by the loch side on the Fast Day, had been drowned. His heart bled for the poor boy cut off in the springtime of his days. But while he owed a duty to the dead, he also owed a duty to the living. He had now to tell them that God was reading to them a terrible warning. Had this unfortunate boy been attending to his duty, had he been at church, had he been observing the day set apart by God's own people, he would still have been in the land of the living and the place of hope. As it was, the punishment fell upon him in the midst of his sin, and without any time for repentance he was sent before the Great Judge. It was an awful thought, but if they believed the Bible it was a thought that they could not help having, that their unfortunate schoolmate was now bitterly repenting his neglect of ordinances in the place of woe."

At the sound of these last three words, horror fell upon the young listeners, and a childish voice was heard calling out, "It's a lee."

"Who said that?" cried the master, white with rage.

"William Torrance," cried the officious Christopher Bain, in a tone of exultation; and, seizing the culprit by the collar, he dragged him forward.

The master took the child by the throat, and shook him. "Now, sir! do you know what you are saying? you are calling, not only my word, by the Word of God a lie. Do you still say that what I said was a lie?"

"It's no true," said Willie, with flashing eyes, and a look of determination on his childish features.

"Then," said the master, taking off his coat and pulling out the *tawse*, "I must punish you, first for the offence, and then I must flog you till you express your regret for what you have said."

Then was witnessed a spectacle which was not uncommon in that class of schools—a man trying to beat what he called "human depravity" out of a child, just as a housemaid beats the dust out of a dirty carpet. But, in this case, the man failed in his task. The boy frequently writhed as the cutting stripes fell upon him; but he shed not a single tear, and kept his teeth resolutely clenched; and at every interval when he was asked if he was not sorry, he kept repeating the phrase, "it's no true." At last the master, puffing and perspiring, was obliged to give in and sit down; and the small culprit stood before him, red and dishevelled, but unsubdued.

"Go out of this school," panted forth, at last, the defeated pedagogue; and the little lad, with a dignity beyond his years, took up his cap and books, walked to the door, and deliberately shut it behind him. He took the same way by which he had come in the early morning; and he carried out his determination not to cry, till at the turning of the road, he unexpectedly caught a glimpse of the loch. Then, before he was aware, an uncontrollable paroxysm of grief came on, and when he arrived at home he was sobbing hysterically. At first, he could not tell his mother what was wrong; and it was only by persistent questioning that she extracted from him all the details of the disaster. She was struck dumb with consternation, and she could only wash his face, brush his hair, and lay him down to rest on her own bed. But when the family assembled at dinner, the horror which his crime excited found expression. "It was an awfu' like thing," said the mother, "to contradick the maister."

"Contradickin' the maister," said the father, "that was the least o't; it was contradickin' the Word o' God "

"I wonder what the neibours will say," skirled the sister, "and Sawbath the Sacrament. I'll never be able to gang forrit."

"It should be threshed oot o' him," growled the brother.

"And that's exactly what I'll dae," said the father; "bring the strap."

The mother, however, was instantly up in arms. She was in general an obedient wife; but here her obedience found its limit. "'Tweel," she cried, "ye'll dae naething o' the kind. The bairn's been hashed enough already. The bluid's barkened on his skin, and his serk's stickin' to his back;" and she took him in her arms as if to protect him.

Next morning his father told him that he must go back to the school and apologise to the master; but that look of determination came again into his youthful face, and he said, "No, I'll no gang." The father got hold of the strap, seized him by the collar, and was about to flog him; but stopped when he said, "Ye may kill me, but I'll no gang." The father was startled and half afraid at this unprecedented rebellion. It was something eerie and uncanny. He did not know what it might lead to. He therefore desisted, and throwing the boy aside, said—

"Weel, I'm through wi' ye. I've dune a' that I can for ye; and if ye gang to the bad, it's yer ain faut. But ye'll no eat the bread o' idleness here. If ye wunna learn ye maun work. Ye maun gang and herd the sheep in the Back Park."

And now was this little fellow made to suffer for his sin. His life must have been very like that of an excommunicated one in the Catholic times. His own father would not speak to him, and would not permit him either to attend church or family worship. The neighbours stared and shook their heads when he passed. His former school-fellows must have been told to avoid him, for they never came near him. The only sympathy he got, if it could be called sympathy, was from "auld Wull Crabbie," the stone-breaker, who plied his hammer near the entrance to the village. This wayside philosopher, shaggy-browed keen-eyed, hook-nosed, perched upon a seat made of an upright stone with a bunch of straw on the top of it, *knapped* away at the "bing" before him; and in the intervals of labour watched all that was going on. From every stranger that passed he levied some bit of information, and to every acquaintance that came near he imparted some sarcastic comment. In fact, he was a cynic, a true follower of Diogenes, scorning the luxuries which never came to him, and finding his true luxury in criticising severely the failings of his fellow-creatures.

One morning when Willie was passing, Wull, fixing his ferret-like eyes upon him, said, "And sae, laddie, ye were bold enough to ca' auld Sloan a leer. Ye stupid shaver, dae ye no ken that dominies and ministers never tell lees. They're perfeck. Did ye ever hear them confess that they were ever wrang? Na! Dod I come to think that they must have been present at the creation, and that they brocht awa wi' them the Mawker's plans, and hae packed them a' into the twa buirds o' the Confession o' Faith. But, toots, what am I sayin'? I'm jist haverin'. Wha am I, to sit in judgment upon men o' that kind? It's aye best to be ceevil, as the auld wife said when she bobbit to the deevil;" and with that he made a fierce blow at a stone and said no more.

For several months Willie continued to be a herd-boy. It was thought a degradation by his father; but he himself felt it to be the reverse. After the bondage and oppression of Sloan's school, what an unspeakable relief it was! He had now the freedom—a freedom which should be the birthright of every young creature—to wander about over the green earth and under the blue sky, to drink in the fresh air and sunshine, to notice all the beauties of beast, and bird, and flower, and to share in the general banquet of joy provided by nature. And another pleasure altogether unexpected awaited him.

One Sunday morning, as he was setting out for the Back Park, his mother said to him that, as it was the Sabbath day, he should take his Bible with him and read it as he herded the sheep. To please her, although the method of his education had given him unpleasant associations connected with the Book, he put it in his pocket; and in the afternoon, as he lay on the grass in a listless mood, he took it out and opened it. Now, it chanced that the passage which caught his eye was the history of Abraham, and before he was almost aware, he was reading it attentively. He could not master some of the hard names and allusions; but he knew enough to understand and appreciate the narrative. Here was a discovery: The Bible, after all, was not a collection of hard names and difficult passages fitted only to puzzle and torment school children. It was a delightful story-book. So he continued to read it day after day. Surrounded as he was with pastoral associations, he dwelt with especial delight on the pastoral scenes in Genesis. In fact, he was never tired of reading them. What a wonderful magic lies in a book which enabled this Scottish shepherd lad in the nineteenth century to enter into the lives and feelings of those primitive shepherd kings of the East! In his own little way he fancied he saw them and heard them speak. He often found himself placing the scenes of the principal events in the pastures that lay before him. For instance, a large beech standing by itself was the tree under which Abraham pitched his tent; a pleasant meadow in the distance was the field where Isaac was meditating at the eventide, when "he lifted up his eyes and saw, and behold, the camels were coming;" and the watering-place at the foot of the Back Park was the well where "Jacob kissed Rachel, and lifted up his voice and wept." This was literally bringing ancient history home to him.

When the winter was coming on, Willie's

mother saw that something must be done for his education. Now, there was in Sandyriggs another school of much higher standing than Sloan's, and the master of it, Mr Fairful, was college-bred, and had the very highest character for intelligence and Christian philanthropy. She, therefore, resolved to apply to him. He was very likely, she thought, to refuse to take her scapegrace, through fear of his contaminating the other children; but at any rate she must do something for the boy. So, one morning, with Willie in her hand, she knocked at the door of the school and asked to see the master. When he came out, he looked so frank, genial, and kind, that she had no hesitation in telling him all about her child.

"I know all about the case," he said. "No doubt the lad was wrong; but those that provoked him were still more to blame. There are certain religious questions so mysterious that they should never be handled, especially before the young. What we have got to do, is to set people on the right road in this world: we should never attempt to fix their everlasting destiny in the next." Then, taking Willie by the hand, and looking at him kindly, he added:

"I'll be happy to receive him, and do what I can for him." Mrs Torrance thanked him warmly, and went away very much relieved.

As time passed on, Mrs Torrance fancied that she saw a change for the better in Willie. He became tidier, and was more particular in washing his face and hands and brushing his hair; and on Sabbath evenings he was often seen reading the Bible. But, on the other hand, very little time seemed to be devoted by him to the preparation of his lessons. On the long winter nights he was usually engrossed with a book, entitled "Natural History of Beasts, Birds, and Fishes," poring over its pages, and copying on paper its pictures of animals; and when the lightsome evenings of spring came, he was almost always out of doors, playing with the tenants of the farmyard, or roving through the woods in search of nests. His big brother, in that masterful tone generally assumed by big brothers, often asked him, "Hoo are ye gettin' on at the schule?" But the invariable answer was "fine." "What dae ye mean by *fine?*" the brother demanded. "Ou, jist fine," was all the reply.

At length came the time when the school

year was to be closed with the public examination. It was a great event; for not only were the pupils to be examined in presence of the public, but the prizes were to be decided on the spot by the voices of the scholars themselves. This method, though common enough in those days, seems to us rough and ready, and apt to lead to favouritism. Yet it seldom failed to arrive at the right decision. The fact was, that the best pupils generally stood out unmistakably; and when there was any doubtful case, the teacher had ways and means of turning opinion in the right direction.

The parents were respectfully invited to be present at this ceremony. Mrs Torrance resolved to go; but it was with fear and trembling. She was afraid that Willie would fail in his examination, and bring disgrace upon her before the public. He was such a queer laddie, and had never brought them anything like credit. And when she went into the schoolroom, and saw the company assembled, her feeling rose to alarm. There were the laird's wife, Mrs Campion, and the parish minister's sister, Miss MacGuffog, and the wife of the principal grocer and of the principal baker, Mrs

Figgins and Mrs Cook, and many others. There were several ministers, black-coated, white-necktied, solemn-faced. Above all there was the Rev. Mr MacGuffog, who had denounced Willie from the pulpit. Oh, what a countenance he had, self-denying and holy without doubt, but oh, so hard and so devoid of ordinary sympathy! There was no saying what this fanatical man might think it his duty to do. He might seize this opportunity of catechising her son and exposing his deficiencies before the assembled company.

The examination, however, went on quietly; and when Willie's class came forward a pleasant surprise awaited her. There was her boy at the top, happy and intelligent, catching encouragement from the teacher's eye, and answering every question. She could not believe that it was the same lad who was so silent, and often so stupid-looking, at home. With flushed cheeks and bright eyes he actually appeared good-looking. His very hair seemed no longer red, but auburn. And when the time came for his class-fellows to award the prizes, there was just one name on their lips, and that was "William Torrance"; and the three rewards, for English,

Bible Knowledge, and Arithmetic respectively, all went to him. And how shall I describe her emotions when the exhibition was over, and all the principal people—Mrs Campion, Mrs Figgins, Mrs Cook, the ministers, and among them Mr MacGuffog himself—came up to congratulate her! The tears were in her eyes, her heart was in her mouth, and she could scarcely frame words wherewith to thank them.

Then the teacher, Mr Fairful, came up, and shaking her hand, told her how gratified he was by Willie's success. "The poor boy," he said, "had been very much misunderstood. He had within him a keen desire to know all about the natural objects around him—human beings, beasts, and birds. Instead of gratifying this desire, those who should have known better tried to cram him with tasks that had no interest for him. The consequence was that he became disgusted, and wore what was considered a sullen and stupid look. But when he came to us, we gave him lessons that were not only interesting, but referred to the familiar scenes around him. Therefore, he devoured them eagerly, and became a most diligent scholar. And then it was that the information about country sights and sounds, which of his own accord he had collected, became of use to him and gave him an advantage over his fellows. A young human soul, in fact, is a rosebud full of delightful possibilities. Keep it in a chilly atmosphere, and it will never develop itself properly, and will very likely become a canker. Surround it with bright and genial influences, and it will gradually open wide its petals, and delight the world with its grace, fragrance, and splendour."

"But, sir, he did not spend much time over his lessons at night."

"No," replied Mr Fairful, "we do not approve of long home lessons. If children give all their attention at school for four or five hours a day, that should nearly be enough. They should then be allowed to enjoy their own freedom, to run about and use their eyes, their limbs, and their lungs, and to learn what their parents and Mother Nature herself can teach them. You need have no anxiety about your son. Leave him to himself, and he will develop his talents in his own way, and if he is spared he will yet be a credit to you."

The master's prophecy was fulfilled. Twenty years afterwards, a lecture on "The Poetry of

Science" was given in Sandyriggs. The lecturer was the eminent professor, Dr William Torrance, from Canada; and the lecture-hall was that very church where he had been denounced as a Boy Heretic.

HOW THE DEACON BECAME AN ABSTAINER.

ABOUT sixty years ago a stranger arrived in the burgh, who at once attracted notice. His name was Mitchell Roper, wholesale brazier; but everyone called him "The Deacon." Why he was called so, nobody knew; and, indeed, nobody inquired, for it was felt that such a special man required a special title.

The truth is that it was his face which at once struck public attention. His face was really his fortune. What his character was, I cannot describe better than by saying, that it was ineffably respectable. Not only all the ten commandments, but all the Christian doctrines, seemed to be written on it. As a natural result, there came very soon to be a demand for it. Those who were getting up a public meeting said to him, "You must give us your countenance." At every public gathering, therefore, it was seen in a prominent place, like the full harvest moon in the sky, or rather (to be more correct) like one of his own copper kettles on a farmer's kitchen wall. And on the mere strength of it, and for no other reason, the Deacon was made, in a very short time, a member of the parochial board, a town councillor, and an elder in the parish church. In this last capacity especially, his influence was potent. Whenever it was his turn to stand at the plate, the collection was nearly double; for when such a sublimely religious visage was regarding them, the members were ashamed to put in the regulation halfpenny. At funerals, too, his presence lent solemnity. The very way in which he partook of the wine that was handed round, gave the company the impression, that he was paying a tribute of respect to the deceased and showing his sympathy with the survivors.

In spite of his popularity, the Deacon, like every other great man, was modest and conciliatory. He had a good word to say about all, especially those in high places. "An excellent man, sir," was the comment which he invariably passed when one of these was mentioned. With him an influential position was like charity: it covered a multitude of sins. He was particularly obsequious to the minister of the parish, Mr Patullo, for he regarded him as the local representative of Church and State, and national institutions generally.

There was one national institution (if we may be allowed to call it so) which the Deacon assiduously kept up, namely, the practice of closing the labours of the day with a tumbler of toddy. Every evening, punctually at ten, as soon as family worship was over and the Bibles were removed, the servant lassie, Eesie, put down on the table whisky, sugar, and hot water. This operation was gone about in such a serious way, that a stranger might have fancied that it was another religious rite which was about to be performed. And if we may judge from the grave manner in which he proceeded to mix the elements, the Deacon evidently thought so too. His wife, indeed, who had not the same reverence for her great husband as the outside world had, tried to limit his allowance of spirits to "one glass and an *eke*." But, as he whispered to himself, he was a sound Whig and could not abide any but Liberal measures. Accordingly, as soon as her back was turned, he dexterously tilted up the bottle and swelled the quantity of spirits; and if she chanced to remark that the colour of the toddy was stronger than usual, he would asseverate in his gravest manner, "only one and an *eke*, my dear." He did not think it necessary to explain that they differed in their notions of the word *eke*. To her mind it meant merely half a glass, to his mind an addition *ad libitum*. A wonderfully accommodating term!

In fact, the Deacon belonged to the old school of worthies commemorated by Lord Cockburn and Dean Ramsay, who practised drinking as a virtue, and who considered whisky as an indispensable necessary of life,—a salve for the body, a balm for the heart, a clarifier for the mind, a solder of friendship, a good omen at births and marriages, and a consolation at funerals. In other words, he was about the last relic of those thorough-going topers who found in almost every circumstance of life a reason for drinking. As he was mixing his toddy he would say, "It is a fine old custom, sir," and then (altering Shakespeare to suit his meaning) he would add, 'A custom more honoured in the observance than in the breach." He had heard of a new-fangled set of men called teetotallers, who condemned drinking on any occasion whatever, but he classed them with those poor creatures—idiots and savages—

who had not yet come into the use of all the blessings of civilisation, and did not know what was good for them. Little did he think that he was destined to become a member of that very body which he so much despised.

The New Year festivities, or, as they were called in Scotland, "the daft days," had come. In Fife, the great day of the feast was Handsel Monday, that is, the Monday after old New Year's Day. It was dedicated to complete relaxation from toil and care, and to the kindly interchange of good wishes and hospitality. Men forgot for a time that they were rivals struggling for existence, and remembered only that they were Christians. They threw off the hard armour of selfishness, and appeared in the guise of charity. Every mansion, every farm-house was turned into a sort of banqueting hall, and was well supplied with comforting viands : oatmeal cakes and cheese for the children, and currant loaves, shortbread, wine and spirits for the adults. No invitations were sent out, but everyone was made heartily welcome. And what a pleasant sight it was to see the merry, chubby-faced tackety-shoed *jockies* and *jennies* going their rounds,—the boys in their well-darned corduroys, the girls in their white *daidlies*, the infants of a year old hoisted on the backs of their brothers, and all carrying pokes to hold the quarter cakes and *whangs* of cheese, which they were sure to get at every farm-town.

Of the adults who kept up these old-fashioned festivities, there was none more faithful than the Deacon. For several years, at Handsel Monday time, he had been accustomed to travel ten miles into the country, starting on Sunday at mid-day, and returning on Tuesday forenoon. His ostensible purpose was to eat his Handsel Monday dinner with one friend, Mr Stark of Kingswell, and his Handsel Monday supper with another friend, Mr Piper of Hallyetts; but he also made it his business to call by the way at many houses, both public and private. Some irreverent wag compared him on these occasions to a Dutch lugger, putting in at every available port for the purpose of victualling; but he felt himself to be a sort of missionary going forth to promote good-will and good-fellowship among men. Sociality, he held, was a virtue which ought to be encouraged for the sake of the dispenser as well as of the receiver. "It is twice blessed: it blesseth him that gives, and him that takes."

On the particular occasion to which this story refers, the Deacon was accompanied by his nephew, Sam Slater. As they set out after forenoon service on a sombre Sunday, they presented a striking contrast. The Deacon was stout, and full and red in the face; Sam was little, and had a lean and hungry look. The Deacon was heavy with a sense of his own dignity; Sam was light and airy as a bird upon the tree. The Deacon was bent upon taking advantage of every possible refreshment by the way; Sam was on the alert to mark the solemn excuses which would be given for this indulgence. It was Bully Bottom led on by tricksy Puck.

They had not gone far before the refreshing process commenced. At the outskirts of the town, when they were passing a small changehouse, the Deacon, giving a shiver, said, "I feel cold; prevention is better than cure; let us fortify ourselves against a chill by a timely dram." And this accordingly they did.

They had travelled four miles, and after climbing a steep hill they had arrived at Baidlin Toll Inn, when the Deacon stopped, and, wiping his perspiring forehead, said, "We must go in here, and cool ourselves with a little of the national beverage."

When they were drinking it, Sam, with a twinkle in his eye, said, "It's strange that we should take our first dram to warm us, and our second to cool us."

"No," replied the Deacon, gravely, "not at all strange; good whisky, sir, is a cure for almost every complaint. It's a sympathetic, comforting friend that fits into all our wants. Yes sir! it fits into all our wants;" and he took a large gulp, and smacked his lips.

The next place of entertainment was at the Cross Roads, three miles farther on. As they came up to it, Sam hurried on and passed the door; but the Deacon, telling him to stop, said, in a voice quavering with emotion, "This house is kept, sir, by a decent woman, Mrs Dowie, who has just lost her husband. It was a sudden call, and my heart bleeds for her. This is not a time to forget the widow and the fatherless. Let us go in, and give her our sympathy." The sympathy was expressed by quaffing two glasses to her very good health.

The only other inn on the way was the well-known house at Inverarden Bridge, near the church and manse.

"Surely," said Sam, as they came up to the

inn, "we need not go in here. This house is not kept by a widow."

"This house," said the Deacon, ignoring the gibe, "was used by my honoured father during his journeys for twenty years, and for his son to pass the door would imply disapproval of his conduct. In these radical times, sir, we should not desert the old paths. Besides," he added, rising into a higher tone, "an inn is a public institution, sanctioned by the magistrates, and paying taxes to uphold the Church and State. As loyal subjects of the King, we must support it."

So in they went, and, fortified by what they imbibed, were able to reach Kingswell, an old-fashioned farm-house surrounded by ancient trees.

That evening the Deacon, with his impressive personality, fairly took possession of the house and its inmates. At tea his face, under the influence of buttered toast, scones, savoury ham, and new-laid eggs, literally shone like a lamp, self-feeding and self-adjusting. Then, seated in the farmer's easy chair beside the fire, he directed the conversation to famous preachers, as a subject appropriate for the evening; and when one minister after another was mentioned, he signified his approval of each by saying, "A workman not needing to be ashamed," or, "A polished shaft in the temple." There was, perhaps, a want of variety about these judgments, but they were uttered with such an air of wisdom that they appeared perfectly conclusive. At nine he "took the Books," and conducted family worship in a manner which satisfied everybody. The servant, Kirstie Clash, whispered to Sam, "He's a wonderfu' man that deacon o' yours. He has eneuch o' unction and command o' Scripter to sair a haill Presbytery." And when he retired for the night, after partaking of a liberal tumbler, it was with the air of a man that had left no duty unperformed.

Next day was one of those mild and sunny gleams that sometimes fall on the sterile landscape of winter, like the memory of some youthful pleasure on the face of an old man. The Deacon rose in the morning like a giant refreshed, and with a giant's appetite.

After a breakfast of ham and eggs and cold fowl, he said to his host, Mr Stark, "By the by, you have a new neighbour at Myreside, Mr Potter. I should like to call upon him."

"Do you know Mr Potter?" asked Mr Stark.

"Not exactly," replied the Deacon, "but he is a relative of my friend, Councillor Tawse."

"Your friend!" exclaimed Sam Slater, in a tone of surprise; "why, Councillor Tawse is your greatest enemy."

"Municipally, but not socially," said the Deacon. "We disagree at the council board, but we make it up at the festive board; and even although he were my enemy, should we not, especially at this season, return good for evil?"

There was no gainsaying this high religious reasoning, and so the Deacon, accompanied by his host and Sam, called at Myreside; and there they were entertained with shortbread, currant loaf, and whisky; and there the Deacon, like a well-oiled machine, performed the conventional task of wishing health and prosperity to the household. But it was at the dinner, which took place at mid-day at Kingswell, where the great man came out in his full strength. After the turkey and plum-pudding, his soul seemed to melt and flow forth in benevolent expression. He proposed toast after toast, he uttered sentiment after sentiment, he christened each toast and sentiment with a liberal libation of toddy, and he got into such a full flow of sociality that it was a difficult task to stop him. At last, when the gloaming was coming on, Sam started up and said that they must set out at once. They were to return homewards by a different road, and stay all night with a hospitable friend, Mr Piper of Hallyetts, who lived at a village half way on their journey.

After a most impressive farewell to Mr Stark and his family, the Deacon took Sam's arm, and proceeded on his way. He had been wound up so tightly by the festivities of the day that he was not yet nearly run down; and as he went on, he descanted warmly upon the hospitalities and virtues of the people they had left. And when Sam, in his own mischievous mood, began to sneer at toast-drinking, and to wonder how the swallowing of liquor could have any effect upon the health and prosperity of other people, the Deacon grew red with righteous indignation.

"Sam," he explained, "I am astonished at your ignorance. The Bible, sir, says that wine maketh glad the heart of man. In other words, it fills the heart with kindly social feeling. This feeling finds its legitimate outlet in kind wishes towards our fellow-men; and what are kind wishes but prayers; and are you such an unbeliever, sir, as to hold that prayers have no effect?"

There was only one public-house by the way; and the whisky which they got there was pronounced by the Deacon to be disgraceful. But he told Sam to cheer up, for they would soon be at a house where they would have every comfort. And then he went off into a eulogy on his friend Piper. "He is a good Samaritan, sir, and his home is a perfect haven of rest; and as for his whisky, it's the balm of Gilead, soothing the wounds of both soul and body."

But, alas for human expectations! When they arrived at Hallyetts, and were welcomed warmly by Mr and Mrs Piper and their family, and when they had been ushered into the dining-room where the table was laid for supper, the Deacon stood aghast. So stands the country gentleman when he steps out of his mansion on a May morning expecting to see nothing but beauty and warmth, and finds the landscape under a sheet of chilling snow. Instead of the warm, heart-cheering decanters that were wont to be there, the Deacon beheld nothing but *cauldrife* bottles of soda water. Was it possible? Was he not mistaken? No, it was too true! The well-remembered, much-comforting Glenlivet was gone! He sank speechless into a chair. He turned red and then white. His friends in alarm gathered round him, asking him if he were ill. He could only whisper, "Brandy, for heaven's sake!"

"I'm very sorry," said Mr Piper, "but we have not a drop of spirits or wine in the house. Did you not hear that we have become abstainers? I thought that all our friends had heard it."

The Deacon could only answer with a look,—a look of pity not unmingled with contempt.

"The fact is," continued Mr Piper, "we were so appalled when our cousin, poor Ned Venters, while under the influence of drink, murdered his wife, that we took the pledge at once."

"Your cousin's vile disposition," said the Deacon, in feeble tones, "was the cause of the crime,—not the drink, unless it was bad. Good sound whisky can't make a man a murderer. It makes him more amiable."

"As Christians," said Mr Piper, "we felt that we were bound to give up strong drink, which causes our brother to err."

"As Christians," retorted the Deacon, still feebly, "we are commanded to celebrate the communion, and while celebrating the communion, we are commanded to drink wine. Your appeal to Christianity won't hold water."

"Come, come, Deacon," said Mr Piper, "have a cup of tea. It will do you more good than brandy, and then you'll go to bed and you'll be all right in the morning."

"No bed for me," murmured the Deacon. "If I was to try to sleep here in my present condition, there would be a *corp* in your house before morning. I'll go home. Come, Sam, we'll find the needed medicine in some humble change-house by the wayside." So saying, the Deacon rose, got his hat, and in a dignified, but (it must be confessed) rather a staggery manner, went out of the house, closely followed by Sam.

Next morning the Deacon awoke with the feeling that he was in unknown quarters. He opened his eyes, and saw that he was in a strange room. For a moment the thought flashed through his brain, "Can this be me?" But the sight of his well-known pantaloons lying on a chair, and in a rather muddy plight, restored his consciousness of personal identity. He rose and looked out at the window, but saw nothing except a few outhouses and a strip of garden, all of which were unfamiliar. He dressed himself hastily, and opened the door of the room, but found himself in a passage where there was no sight or sound of anybody. He crept quietly along, and finding a room door open, entered it. There was no one in it. It was evidently a parlour, bright and comfortable, with a clear fire in the grate, and with the walls covered with numerous pictures and sketches. And what was this paper on the table? It was a sketch of a figure. He took it up; and, could he believe his eyes? Yes! rough and hasty though it was, it was a representation of himself in a state of stupor—hair dishevelled, eyes swollen and closed, features distorted, mouth open, jaw hanging down; and underneath it was written "A Drunken Sot." Could this be the countenance of which he was so proud, and which, his admirers said, was the embodiment of respectability? As he looked at it, he felt that his good name was gone, and the perspiration fell in drops from his forehead. What enemy could have done this?

He was still wondering, when steps were heard approaching, and he had just time to push away the picture, when there stood in the doorway the very last man whom at that moment he would have wished to see—the Rev. Mr Patullo. And this gentleman behaved in an extraordinary manner. Not a smile of recognition did he give. Not a word did he utter. He merely sat down and gazed sorrowfully on the Deacon. His feelings were evidently too strong for words. The silence continued for about a minute. It was an awful minute for the Deacon. He felt that he ought to speak; but he really could not do it till he knew where he was; and it would be a most humiliating question to ask, " Where am I ? "

At last the minister broke the oppressive silence. In that slow, deep, and funereal tone for which he was famous, he repeated again and again just one word—" Lost! Lost! Lost!" and then stopped. This was a favourite method of his, which he often used at the beginning of his sermon, and which at once riveted and solemnised his congregation. And on this occasion it sounded in the Deacon's ears like the voice of Doom. Then after an awful pause, the minister continued:

"This is terrible, Mr Roper, terrible for me, and still more terrible for you. I came here yesterday to dine and stay the night with my friend, Mr Virtue, the artist. We were sitting at supper, when intelligence arrived that a gentleman of respectable appearance had dropped down by the roadside, and that his friend who was with him was unable to take him any farther. He was brought in, and you may imagine what was my horror when I found that the gentleman was my friend and chief elder, and that he was in a plight which I can't trust myself to describe. Now, as I must bring this matter before the Kirk Session—"

"Oh! Mr Patullo, you surely will never do that."

"I must. I would be quite unworthy of my place if I did not do it. If it were not your own case, you yourself would advise that. You remember how severe you were upon poor Willie Flett, who was up before us last month. But before I make up my mind definitely, I shall listen to any explanation you have to give."

The Deacon, fortunately for himself, had long cultivated the faculty of putting the best face on every matter, and this faculty now served him in good stead. So, shaking Mr Patullo's hand, and wiping a tear from his eye, he said, " Thank you, sir, you are acting as my best friend, as you have always done. I will, therefore, tell you frankly the whole matter. Sam Slater and I were keeping our Handsel Monday at Kingswell.

I am not an abstainer, as you know, and have always used the gifts of Providence without abusing them. At dinner I had my share of the punch, but no more, and when we set out I was perfectly well. But, unfortunately, at a half-way house where we stopped for refreshment, the whisky was bad. As soon as I had taken it, I felt ill, and said so to Sam. It was some time before it acted; but at length it made me quite sick and helpless. Mr Patullo! it was poison and not drink that put me into such a sad condition! I was really ill, not intoxicated."

Mr Patullo hummed and hawed, and said, "Would you object to me hearing what Mr Sam Slater has got to say?"

"Nothing would gratify me more," said the Deacon, although he did not look as if he were gratified. The fact is, that he was not sure on what line the whimsical Sam might get.

When Sam came in and was asked point blank by the minister, "How do you account for the state in which Mr Roper was last night?" it seemed as if he were going to put his foot into it. Blushing and hesitating he said, "Well! really I could not undertake to say." But when the minister asked him if they got anything at the roadside public-house which disagreed with them, he saw what cue he was to take.

"Ah! yes," he said, brightening up, "I remember now — the bad whisky. The Deacon, after drinking it, said that it was atrocious. It had no bad effect at first; but when we were in Mr Piper's house, I noticed that the Deacon turned as white as a sheet, and when we came out into the open air, he became so sick that he had to sit down by the wayside. Yes, it must have been the adulterated drink that poisoned him."

"But how was it that you were not poisoned?" asked the minister.

"For the simple reason," answered Sam, "that I merely put the stuff to my lips and did not take off my glass."

"Well," said the minister, after some anxious consideration, "as a Christian pastor I must take the most charitable view; and even as a humane man, I must, where there is a doubt, give the accused the benefit of a doubt. I therefore will agree to make no charge against you. But you must take means instantly to prevent yourself ever falling into such suspicious circumstances again."

"How can I do that?" asked the Deacon.

"By taking the pledge," replied the minister: "not publicly—just now at least, that might rouse people's suspicion, but privately to myself. I shall draw up a paper here to-day, which you will sign, and to which Mr Slater will append his name as a witness. I shall then explain to the people of the house that you were ill, not intoxicated, and that to prevent the uncharitable world putting the worst construction on the circumstance, they must mention this lamentable occurrence to nobody."

But the Deacon demurred, and turned sick at the idea of taking the pledge. What! he who had upheld moderate drinking as the right use of the mercies of Providence, and had branded total abstainers as casting a reflection on Him who turned water into wine!

Mr Patullo, however, in a resolute voice said, "Mr Roper, if you could have seen yourself as others saw you last night—but what is this?" He had caught sight of the sketch on the table, had taken it up and was looking at it. "This is the work of Tom, Mr Virtue's son. He is an art student, and sketches everybody and everything. It was too bad of him to take advantage of you in your unfortunate plight. But its turning up just now, at this critical moment, serves a good purpose. It gives you the power which Burns so much desired for mankind—the power of seeing yourself as others see you. Look at it, Mr Roper, and listen to me. What happened yesterday may happen again in your own town. You may take a glass too much, and that glass, like the one that has made you ill, may be poison. And what will be the result? You will appear before your fellow-townsmen, your fellow-Christians, your own wife, in this disgusting condition. Your ruin will then be instant and irretrievable. The high character which you have maintained for so many years will fall to pieces; and from being the respected and admired of Sandyriggs society, you will become, what you are represented here to be, 'a drunken sot.'"

The Deacon shuddered at the prospect thus held up before him, and seizing Mr Patullo's hands, declared that he was ready to sign a promise, renouncing drink for ever.

The Deacon was able to keep his promise; for, if he ever felt tempted to stretch forth his hand towards the enchanted cup, the thought of that horrible sketch appalled him and quenched the desire. He now gave his countenance to every teetotal platform; and if that countenance had lost the florid complexion which at one time had been so much admired, yet it still beamed with wisdom. He seldom spoke, but his silence was far more expressive than his speech would have been. His usual luck also attended him. He was now pointed out as a fine specimen of a self-sacrificing Christian, one who had given up all the delights of convivial society, of which he was a great favourite, in order to set an example to his weaker brethren.

THE END.

Printed by M'FARLANE & ERSKINE, *Edinburgh.*

www.ingramcontent.com/pod-product-compliance
Lightning Source LLC
Chambersburg PA
CBHW031349230426
43670CB00006B/484